16 and a half WAYS TO UPGRADE YOUR FAITH

BOB WALLINGTON

16 and a half WAYS TO UPGRADE YOUR FAITH

First published in Great Britain in 2019

Society for Promoting Christian Knowledge
36 Causton Street
London SW1P 4ST
www.spck.org.uk

British Library Cataloguing-in-Publication Data
A catalogue record for this book is available from the British Library

ISBN 978–0–281–07879–0
eBook ISBN 978–0–281–07880–6

1 3 5 7 9 10 8 6 4 2

Typeset by Manilla Typesetting Company
First printed in Great Britain by Jellyfish Print Solutions
Subsequently digitally reprinted in Great Britain

eBook by Manilla Typesetting Company

Produced on paper from sustainable forests

To Mike Pilavachi, Will Kemp, Paul Daniels, Beki Watson, Mike Maddox, Phil Maddox, Andy Sachs, Melissa Sorrill, Ruth Daborn, Lucy Thomas and Mark Russell. The youth leaders who got to know me, walked with me, encouraged me, loved me and showed me more of what it looked like to live for Jesus.

To the young people I have had the privilege of serving over the years. Despite the fact that you have tested my patience, robbed me of sleep, cost me a lot of money and occasionally caused me to cry, my life has been so much richer as a result of knowing each of you. I love you guys very much.

CONTENTS

FOREWORD

This is an absolute gem of a book. There are many reasons why I say this. Here are some of them.

First, when I begin to read a book, I want to know about the author. What is he or she like? Does what he or she has to say have integrity? In other words, does the author's life confirm or contradict his or her teaching? I have known Bob Wallington for years – in fact, since he was 11! He is a man of compassion, kindness, humility, faithfulness and has a huge servant heart. You can be assured that what you read in these pages has been lived out and is not theory copied from other writings. Bob has been a brilliant youth pastor in our church – loving, encouraging and challenging our young people to rise up and live wholeheartedly for Jesus. I have watched him make extraordinary sacrifices for the sake of those he leads and never draw attention to that fact.

Second, this book is practical. Brilliantly practical. It covers all the bases. Prayer, church, reading the Bible, relationships, attitudes, stepping out, community . . . It is all there. Bob clearly explains how to do the Christian life without religious jargon and provides brilliant illustrations and examples from his own and others' lived experience. There have been many moments as I have read these pages when I wanted to shout, YES! There are so many suggestions for how we can put this teaching into practice in accessible and practical ways.

Third, this book is rooted in Scripture and draws out teachings from the Bible that are pure genius. Bob takes passages that I have read hundreds of times and points out truths in them that left me wondering, 'Why didn't I see that?' In fact, this book will give you a renewed hunger to read the Bible, which is a necessary and welcome gift to this generation.

Fourth, this book drips wisdom. This may seem a strange thing to say, but I believe wisdom is a neglected virtue in our day. Wisdom results from a mixture of revelation, contemplation and suffering. Wisdom is a gift given to the humble rather than the clever. That is why it is so rare. This book, like its author, has wisdom in spades.

I say again, this is a gem of a book. I commend it to you.

Mike Pilavachi

ACKNOWLEDGEMENTS

A few years back, I was giving a seminar at a Soul Survivor summer festival in a large, barn-like structure filled with young people and the lingering smell of the cows that had been there the previous week! In the seminar, I was unpacking a number of practical things that the young people could put into practice to enable their faith to flourish when they returned home from the festival.

Afterwards, I was approached by a brilliant lady called Juliet Trickey, who floated the idea of turning the content of that seminar into a book. Despite my surprise and hesitations, as I had never written a book before, she encouraged me to give it a go. Along the way she has been a well of enthusiasm and support and without her this would never have been a finished book. She has been gracious and understanding over missed deadlines, come up with excellent suggestions and just been a dream to work with. Thank you also to Nicki Copeland, who brilliantly edited the manuscript, and to all the team at SPCK, who have helped turn my mumblings into something more.

I couldn't have written this book without the family at Soul Survivor Watford cheering me on and encouraging me.

Mike Pilavachi and Andy Croft – I love working with you and for you. Your jokes are as horrendous as your friendship, leadership and encouragement are wonderful! Thank you also, Mike, for writing the foreword, despite being ridiculously busy!

Zoe Lowe and Tabi Wallington, in your roles working with the young people at Soul Survivor Watford, you both have carried more so that I could write this book. I love working with you and have so appreciated talking through much of the content of this book with you as I have been writing it. Your insights, expertise and wisdom are woven into so much of this book.

Finally, and above all, I want to thank Tabi, Phoebe and Libby for being such hilarious, adventurous and joy-filled sources of inspiration, encouragement and laughter throughout all the highs and lows of writing this book. I love you so much.

INTRODUCTION

I've been a Christian since I was about eight years old. Which means that, for a couple of decades, I have been trying to work out what it means to follow Jesus. If you were to ask me to describe this journey, I would definitely use the word 'roller coaster'.

I grew up hating roller coasters. Even before I had ever been on one, I hated them. I was afraid of the heights, the speed, the loops and the bends, but most of all, of not being able to get off it once I was strapped in! When I was 14, some friends and I went to a theme park while we were on holiday in America. I spent the whole day holding everyone else's stuff while they queued and flew round the tracks on these giant, incredible . . . INSANE roller coasters. I stood there watching their faces fly by, displaying a mix of intense fear and enjoyment all at the same time. Some of them screamed; others were entirely quiet, just trying to keep it together; others were abandoned, lifting their hands into the resistance of the wind just to be sure they were moving at ludicrous speeds. And there I was, watching, quietly wanting to join in. But, as they roared past, doing another 12 spirals, I was also fairly happy to be the bag boy.

The first time anyone actually got me on a roller coaster was when I was 18. We were at Alton Towers, a theme park in Cheshire in the UK, and I was helping on a camp that our church was running for 11–14-year-olds. I had my small group with me – a bunch of seven or eight tough, mean, brutish 13-year-old boys. These guys had been talking all week about the roller coasters. They bragged about how many roller coasters they had conquered in the past, which ones were the scariest, fastest, had the most complete loops, etc., etc. I didn't contribute much to the conversations/bragging sessions, as you can imagine. Anyway, the day came, the buses arrived at camp and off we went. When we arrived at the park, it seemed like seconds before me and my boys were stood in the queue for the main attraction at the time: 'Oblivion'. Now, there's something ironic about being at a Christian camp all week, singing love songs to Jesus, being filled with his Spirit, resting in his presence, only to then, on the last day, face OBLIVION! Nice way to wrap up the week!

Anyway, all of a sudden, the lads and I were moving to fill up the area where you wait when you are next on the ride. I started to panic. What do I do? What do I tell the lads? What will they think of me? I blurted out something like, 'Enjoy this one guys. I'll look after your stuff.' That had worked in the past in America. But not this time. They looked at me like a piece of old chewing gum they'd just found underneath the desk at school. Then it all goes blank. No, I didn't faint, but

I have no recollection of what happened next and how I got on the ride, but I did. And the lads were loving it. Especially as we lurched forwards and the giant seated platform began to crank its way slowly upwards. Up and up and up it went, for what seemed like an eternity. And then, as we reached the top, we glided forwards. All seemed fairly tranquil until a creepy voice from a speaker somewhere sounded out, 'Don't. Look. Doooooown!' and the whole platform jolted forwards so that we were now at 90 degrees, hanging there, staring down into, well . . . OBLIVION! I prayed, I confessed and I prepared myself to meet my maker. Then they let the brakes off and we plummeted down and down and down.

As you may have worked out, we made it back to camp alive and, to be completely honest, after that moment I began to love roller coasters. I went on all of them that day and we rode Oblivion at least twice more!

But as I have come to love roller coasters and experience the thrills that they bring, the huge heights and spectacular lows, the rolls and loops and bends and sudden twists and turns, it all reminds me of what it can be like to follow Jesus.

One minute you're on top of the world (often at a Christian festival or worship event), life following Jesus seems so great, straightforward and you feel like you're winning at this 'being a Christian' thing, and then suddenly . . . JOLT! Out of nowhere: 'Don't. Look. Doooooown!' and you find yourself a million miles from that other place, questioning, doubting, getting stuff wrong and maybe even wanting to walk away from your faith altogether. Then somehow you get back on track as you see (insert name of Christian festival or worship event here) fast approaching, you're heading up, up, up, and you reach the top again and it feels like you're on top of the world, life following Jesus is great, you're winning and then . . . JOLT! 'Don't. Look. Doooooown!' Repeat. Repeat. Repeat.

Maybe you can relate to a faith that feels like it rolls from one Christian event to the next, with huge gaps in the middle where it all goes downhill, where you can't seem to find the same intimacy with God, hear his voice as clearly or understand what you're reading in the Bible any more?

If your walk with Jesus is anything like mine was in my teenage years, then this might be a pattern you recognize. And if you do feel like that, then this book is going to help you, because there's another way to do life with Jesus. In John's Gospel, Jesus says, 'I have come that they [that's us!] may have life, and have it to the full' (John 10.10). Don't you want to explore what Jesus is talking about there? The idea of living a 'full' life or experiencing 'life to the full' excites me! I want to live that life and to experience everything that comes with following Jesus into fullness of life.

When we look at Jesus' life, it was full of ups and downs and twists and turns – a real roller coaster (especially the three years we see in greater detail in the Gospels) – but in the midst of that, his relationship with the father wasn't like that – it was stable and steadfast.

The tips in this book are all about helping you to develop your own stable and steadfast faith amid your own ups and downs, twists and turns. Putting these tips into action won't mean that you'll avoid the struggles or heartaches of the lows, but it will help you navigate them and learn from them, all the while deepening your relationship with Jesus. Here are 16 (and-a-half) ways to see your walk with Jesus deepen and grow in your everyday, normal life.

BEGIN HERE

So where do you start if you want to break free of the same old routines and patterns that you've always lived and discover a new reality? Where on earth is the best place to begin? The answer is: inside you. Literally, that's where you have to start if you want to go the distance; it all has to begin with a passion in your heart.

Why does it have to start with your heart? Because otherwise it's just someone else telling you that 'you should do this thing or that'. Eventually, if it's just someone else's good idea or advice or suggestion, all of us run out of steam when we try to implement it in our own lives. Well, that's my experience anyway. It's like healthy eating. If someone tells you to start eating more healthily, suggesting you eat less sugar and more vegetables, its long-term effectiveness is limited. But if *you* really want to start eating healthily, to steer clear of the sugar and to try to up your intake of fruit and vegetables, you're much more likely to see a difference.

Unless *you* actually want the change, unless there is a passion inside *you* for a new reality, the fuel that you need to succeed just isn't there.

Michael Schumacher, the famous Formula 1 driver, once said, 'Once something is a passion, the motivation is there.'[1]

So, you may be reading this and thinking, 'But how do I get a passion for this new way of living?'

The liberating truth is that you don't have to clench your fists, grit your teeth and conjure it up out of somewhere. All you need to do is ask God, by his Holy Spirit, to give you that passion. Then you have to trust that God has given it to you (even if you don't feel any different right away) and begin to take some initial small steps forwards.

I often speak to young people who know Jesus and want to follow him, but they, like many of us, struggle sometimes to find a passion to live differently and make some of the tough decisions that following Jesus requires us to. Living differently in this world is so hard. We can talk about it in church or youth group like it's easy, but it just isn't. It's so hard to be the one person in your friendship group who is making choices that no one else understands. Take the 'going to church thing' as an example. To choose to get up early and go to church on a Sunday morning when all your school friends are going shopping together or your sports team has an important game is incredibly hard. It takes a huge amount of motivation

1 Maurice Hamilton, 'Schumacher keeps his foot down', *The Guardian*, 24 February 2002.

and strength to live differently in this world, so where do we get that passion and energy to live differently from? The Holy Spirit is the only one who can breathe this into your heart.

Living a life that is growing more into the likeness of Jesus is impossible if we're trying to do it by ourselves. We need the Holy Spirit to help us. Trying to do it without him is like trying to make bread without flour. You need him because he's the essential ingredient. He's the purest, best, most-powerful and distinctly different-from-anything-else-in-this-world ingredient. But we also need each other. The Church is far more than a building. It is a group of people who want to grow into the likeness of Jesus together and to do the things Jesus did. Encouragement from our church family is like the yeast in the dough.

Why don't you take a minute to think about that? Ask God to help you. Ask yourself the question, 'If my relationship with Jesus were to grow this year, what are the things that would change in my everyday life?'

Sometimes it's helpful to think about a few key areas. What would these areas of your life look like in a year's time if you were to really go for it with God?

- Engaging with the Bible: reading/listening/memorizing (maybe you find reading it really difficult and by this time next year you want to be reading one verse every day. Maybe there's a particular book you want to read through . . .).

- Prayer life: speaking to God and listening to him.
- Church and youth group: how often are you there and how do you engage if you are there?
- Relationships with your family and friends.

Relationship

Now that we've talked about the motivation, let's talk about what we're actually trying to achieve.

The thing we need to remember from the very beginning is that our aim (and God's desire) is to grow in our relationship with Jesus. It's not about becoming a 'better Christian' or achieving some kind of higher level as a follower of Jesus. God's heart for each of us is that we would want to grow closer to him.

I am sure you have heard before that 'Christianity is not a religion; it is a relationship.' Following Jesus is not about a set way of worshipping, rules to adhere to or living by a list of 'can do this, but can't do that'. The God of the Bible reveals himself as a God of three: he is Father, Son and Holy Spirit, and in his very nature he is relational. So as we draw near to him and he draws near to us, we are brought into this relationship.

Moses is a great example of this. Find him in the Old Testament if you don't know his story. He goes on the most amazing adventure of growing his relationship with God. On the way, Moses discovers that his God (and therefore his life) is all about liberation and freedom. Moses meets God in the burning bush on Mount Sinai (Exodus 3) and the conversation goes like this:

> **'Moses! Moses!'**
> **And Moses said, 'Here I am.'**
> **'Do not come any closer,' God said. 'Take off your sandals, for the place where you are standing is holy ground.' Then he said, 'I am the God of your father, the God of Abraham, the God of Isaac and the God of Jacob.' At this, Moses hid his face, because he was afraid to look at God. (Exodus 3.4–6)**

Do you see how the relationship began between God and Moses? Moses hid his face because he was afraid to look at God. If you turn to 30 chapters later in your Bible, there is a beautiful line that describes the journey their relationship took over the years:

> **The LORD would speak to Moses face to face, as one speaks to a friend. (Exodus 33.11)**

That is beautiful. Their relationship went from being one where Moses hid his face from God to being one where he would speak with God face to face, as one speaks to a friend. I love that image!

Peter, in the New Testament, goes on a similar journey. At their first meeting, Jesus gets into Peter's boat and tells him to try fishing again (after Peter and his companions had not caught anything all night). So they let down the nets and they catch so many fish that the boat begins to sink. They call over another boat and fill both boats so full that they too begin to sink. They have never seen anything like it. EVER! We read that Peter falls to his knees (in awe and fear) and says, 'Go away from me, Lord; I am a sinful man!' (Luke 5.8). Peter's response to meeting God is to tell him to go away!

Then, after spending three years with Jesus and journeying with him, ministering with him, hearing his words, seeing his miracles, joining in with his miracles, seeing the arrest, crucifixion, death and then resurrection of Jesus, Peter finds himself fishing in a boat again (John 21) and, in a similar way to before, they are out all night and don't catch anything. Then they hear a man call out from the beach, 'Throw your net on the right side of the boat and you will find some.' When they did, the catch of fish was miraculous, just like it had been at Peter's first encounter with Jesus. They realize the man on the beach calling out to them is not a stranger: it's Jesus. Peter is so excited that he jumps out of the boat! He swims to shore out of this longing to be near Jesus.

I love these two stories that talk to us about relationship with God. Both Moses and Peter begin a relationship with God in fear, wanting to hide, but both men go on the adventure of becoming friends with God. Moses goes from covering his face to speaking with God face to face, and Peter goes from asking Jesus to get out of his boat to a place where he is jumping out of the boat in sheer desperation and joy at being in the presence of his friend and his God.

As they become friends with the one in whose image they were made, both these men discover more about that image. The same is true for you and me: we find the best, purest, truest, most free and exciting version of ourselves when we become friends with God.

This is the kind of friendship that I believe God wants with you. Everything else you discover about yourself is a bonus!

Relationship with God is the most crucial, fundamental part of upgrading your faith. No one can do it for you and it doesn't always feel easy, but it will provide the most awesome foundation from which you can live your life.

I have tried to build into this book a number of very practical, easy things that you can do to help take your faith to the next level when you get home from a Christian event. None of it, though, makes any sense without the foundation of a relationship with Jesus. No matter how many of these practical tools you utilize, knowing God and growing daily in the adventure of knowing him is what it's all about. Every practical tool in this book is to help that relationship continue, grow and flourish.

> 'I am the good shepherd; I know my sheep and my sheep know me.' (John 10.14)

> 'I no longer call you servants, because a servant does not know his master's business. Instead, I have called you friends, for everything that I learned from my Father I have made known to you.' (John 15.15)

#1

ASK THE HOLY SPIRIT TO FILL YOU EACH MORNING

Arriving home after a Christian conference or other event can be a weird thing. Some of us won't have seen the news for days; we feel a little disconnected from the 'real world' and what's been happening. We see family and friends, reconnect with our routines, enjoy some of the comforts that home brings. The introverts among us find rest in a space that's away from the crowds; the extroverts reminisce about the energy-ball of people that they were entangled with only a few hours ago.

As we return to our homes and the life-changing moments of the past few days/weeks replay in our memories, it can feel a little lonely. We may even feel like suddenly we're on our own and it's up to us to carry on sustaining the deeper level of intimacy with Jesus we may have experienced while we were away.

That is not actually true.

Closer than you could imagine, there is a friend who's there to help you. The Holy Spirit is a person and he lives and dwells in the hearts of God's children. Sometimes we forget he's there, which seems crazy when we start to understand who he really is.

Jesus talked about him to his disciples. He said:

> **'I will ask the Father, and he will give you another helper who will be with you forever. That helper is the Spirit of**

> **Truth. The world cannot accept him, because it doesn't see or know him. You know him, because he lives with you and will be in you.' (John 14.16–17, GW)**

The Holy Spirit is our helper. He is living with you and in you, so that you are never alone. You do not have to work out how to 'live the Christian life' on your own or even do it by your own grit and determination (although at times it will require a lot of grit and determination!) The Holy Spirit has come to live with you and in you to help you do what is otherwise impossible.

When I was about 15, I remember hearing a talk by a rather large and eccentric Greek man, called Mike Pilavachi, who I am now very privileged to call a friend (and also boss!) I remember him saying:

> **To live the Christian life isn't just hard; it's not difficult . . . It's IMPOSSIBLE!**

He paused for a minute to let that sink in. I remember thinking, 'Well, what on earth are we all doing here then?!' Then he took the time to explain to us that the supernatural life Jesus calls us to as his disciples is only possible through the Holy Spirit.

When things in my life have felt dry and stale or when living the Christian life feels like a back-breaking uphill struggle, I often reflect that I have forgotten the 'helper' that I so desperately need to make this whole thing come alive. It just doesn't work when we try to do it in our own strength, rather than in the power of the Holy Spirit.

A few years ago, I felt that God was telling me to give up my job and go to live in South Africa for a short time. About three weeks before I was due to get on a flight to Cape Town, I remember walking into an empty church building before anyone else arrived for the service. I sat down and started to talk to God about all the things that were 'missing' from my 'get this sorted before you leave' list. I had nowhere to live when I got there, no specific job to do, no money to live on for the length of time I wanted to be there, no means of transportation, no friends, no idea about how I would know how to get around once I was there. As I sat there in that empty church building, I asked God, 'Please can you sort these things out for me, Lord? I know you want me to go, but I don't want to go unless I've got these things sorted.'

I remember feeling his answer resound in my heart . . . 'No, Bob.'

I couldn't believe it! 'Why, Lord?! Why won't you sort these things out for me?'

Then I just felt God say to me, 'I will be with you. I will be all that you need. I will be your bank manager, I'll be your tour guide, I'll be your estate agent, I'll be your friend. With me, anything is possible.'

I often look back on that moment as a reminder that so often in my life I try to make things happen in my own strength, but it is never as good (or as exciting!) as when we let the Holy Spirit run the show.

In the book of Acts, we see that when the Holy Spirit fills the disciples, it's not as a one-off single deposit, but it happens multiple times (see Acts 2.4; 4.8; 4.31; 13.52). When the Holy Spirit fills the disciples and the other followers of Jesus in these accounts, it is usually followed by some kind of action. Sometimes these actions are miraculous, like when Peter and John tell a man who has been lame since birth to 'get up and walk!' (and he does! Acts 3.6–8). At other times the Holy Spirit fills them to enable them to speak about Jesus in amazing ways (in other languages or just with incredible power). Sometimes, when the Holy Spirit fills the disciples, they are empowered with a supernatural boldness to proclaim who Jesus is, despite the threats of beatings, imprisonment and sometimes death that have been made against them.

So how do we keep on being filled with the Holy Spirit as we return home? Try this . . .

Each morning when you wake up, take a minute to pray and ask God to fill you afresh with the Holy Spirit so that you can live the life he's called you to.

#2

SHOW UP . . .
EVERY TIME!

Show up . . . every time.

To what?

Church.

And . . .

Youth group.

If you were expecting some incredibly profound, deep, intellectual and theological bombshell to be dropped here, then think again. Sometimes in our humanness we fail to see where the real power is. But let me assure you of this: there is power in committing to God's people.

Commitment is cheap these days. I mean, so much of what we think is commitment isn't really commitment at all. We live in a culture that doesn't want to 'sign on the dotted line' in case something better comes along. This attitude seeps into friendships, parties, relationships, marriages – and, of course, the Church is not exempt from this. There are more opportunities than ever before to engage our passions and interests, hobbies and pastimes, and let's not forget the academic pressures of school! It seems like everything wants your attention, your energy, your time . . . your commitment.

So the issue at hand is priorities. What in your life are you going to make a priority? What are you going to decide is most important to you?

When I was a lot younger and my parents weren't Christians, my identical twin brother, Sam, and I spent our Sunday mornings playing football for our local Sunday League team. We loved football. I remember after one match, my mum and dad told us that the opposition manager was going crazy about how much ground 'that Wallington kid' was covering. He hadn't realized that there were two of us on the pitch! Sam and I played for several teams, including this one on Sundays. And then (in what seemed like a flash) my parents became Christians; they encountered God and it changed everything (mostly in wonderful ways). Then, one Saturday afternoon, Mum and Dad sat us down and explained that, as a family, they felt it was important for us to be together in church on Sunday mornings and to make that a priority over everything else, so we could only play for our Sunday team if the games were in the afternoon. Sam and I were upset, but we soon got over it and, now, that decision my parents made on our behalf rings in my ears as one of the most important decisions they ever made, because it showed me how important they felt it was to commit to meeting with God's people and to make sacrifices that were about putting God first in our lives. They were willing to upset us, even though they loved us so much and wanted us to be happy, because they wanted us to know what was truly important.

You may have heard of the famous runner Eric Liddell or even the film *Chariots of Fire* that was made about him. In the 1920s, he ended up playing rugby for Scotland and also qualifying for the Olympic Games that were to be held in Paris in 1924. He was a sprinter, particularly good at running the 100 metres. When he got to the Olympic Games in Paris, he found out that the heats for the 100 metres were held on a Sunday. Even though he wasn't at home in Edinburgh, he still wanted to set aside Sundays as a day to be together with God's people and in church, so he decided not to compete, despite being the favourite to win the gold medal. He discovered that the 400 metres heats were held on another day and decided to enter that distance instead of the 100 metres, for which he'd trained for so long. He ended up getting through the qualifiers and into the final of the 400 metres.

Sir Arthur Marshall, who was one of Liddell's friends and fellow Olympians, wrote this about the 400 metres final:

> **The silence and pent-up excitement at the start of the race could be felt. Liddell went ahead at the start and**

> maintained his pace throughout, finishing in what at the time was described as 'a most lion-hearted manner' winning by three yards from Fitch, an American. This was probably the greatest achievement of the VIIIth Olympiad, and superlatives were showered on Liddell by the press of the entire world.[2]

Eric Liddell broke the 400-metre world record not just once . . . but three times during qualifying and in the final.

It emerged in later years that, just before the 400 metres final, Eric Liddell was slipped a small scrap of paper by an American athlete. On it were the words from 1 Samuel 2.30: 'Those who honour me I will honour.'

What we commit to in life is what we prioritize. When Tabi and I made our marriage vows, we committed our lives to each other (with God at the centre) and so we prioritize our relationship. I don't spend more time with my mates than I do with Tabi and she doesn't spend more time at the gym than she does with me. We've committed to each other and so our marriage, and keeping it healthy, is a priority.

---

2 'Recollections of Eric Liddell by Sir Arthur Marshall', Eric Liddell Cnter. Available online at: <www.ericliddell.org/about-us/eric-liddell/1924-olympics> (accessed 20 February 2019).

If you're not sure what or who you're committed to, then work backwards through the equation. What are you prioritizing in your life? Is it schoolwork/grades, maybe work or that much-loved Xbox? Is it how many Instagram likes you're getting, the friends you have at school, earning some cash or perfecting those musical skills? Are you committed to the things that draw you closer to Jesus?

What about making church and youth group a priority?

#3

FIND YOUR GREEN ARMCHAIR

When I started my first-ever paid job in youth ministry, it came with a house. It was a beautiful little cottage on the edge of the town and, when I moved in, the previous youth pastor had left me a few bits of furniture (very kind indeed!) One of those pieces of furniture was an old, green armchair. That green armchair had seen better days, but it was still pretty comfy and it wasn't like I was used to having my own house – I barely had any furniture of my own to put in it – so I kept it and put it in the corner of my bedroom.

I sat in that green armchair almost every morning, shortly after I woke up, with my bowl of cereal and a good old cup of tea. I was in the habit of spending some time each morning with Jesus and it just so happened that this green armchair was a pretty comfortable place to do that. I would often open up my Bible, read for a while, maybe write down in a journal a few things that I thought God was saying to me through his word, then plug in my headphones and spend some time listening to some worship music and praying.

After a while, I came to realize, that moment was, in some ways, the most important part of my day. It was important because it set the direction I would walk in and the way in which I would walk. It was like being reminded or recalibrated each morning with a sense of the big picture – the love of God. In particular, I often found that things I would read from the Bible would almost jump up into my memory at different points in the day. Sometimes remembering the scripture would encourage me into action: a moment of generosity or an act of kindness. At other times the passage that would jump back into my head during the day would help me in a moment of worry or nervousness.

When we open up the Scriptures, we see that even Jesus (who is God) took time regularly to be with the Father. Luke 5.16 says, 'But Jesus often withdrew to lonely places and prayed.' And if Jesus needed to do that, how much more must we need that!

The thing is, though, this isn't all that easy. I mean, on paper it's simple and, as you're reading this, you may even be thinking, 'Yeah, I can do that', but once you get started actually doing it, you might find it's actually pretty hard. You may have to set your alarm to wake you up 15 minutes earlier in the morning or find some time later in the day if the morning is not your thing or stay awake for a bit longer to meet with God before your head hits the pillow in the evening. Then there are the added distractions of that wonderful bit of smart technology that is semi-stuck to your hand, that last-minute piece of homework that you need to finish, that chapter in the book you're reading that is screaming at you, 'READ ME!!', that friend who's spammed you with messages, desperate for your reply, the endless stream of photos or posts that crave your attention on social media or that cute guy/girl who's sending you flirty texts. It can feel like an absolute battle just to carve out a short amount of time in the day to be still and spend some time with God.

That, my friends, is where we need to wake up to the fact that you and I are in a spiritual battle. There is an enemy out there trying desperately to stop you growing and deepening your relationship with Jesus and to stop you spending time with him each day. I don't say that to worry you; I say it so that you are more aware of his agenda and can spot when things are drawing you away from meeting with God.

The fact that there are so many distractions drawing us away from spending time with Jesus should also wake us up to the potential power and significance of this time with him! The place of greatest persecution is often the place of greatest promise in our lives. I have found over the years that the hardest time to protect in my daily walk with God is the time in my green armchair where I meet with him and sit at his feet and where our relationship grows deeper and deeper. It would make sense for the enemy to target these moments and throw every distraction he can at them each day, because he knows that they have the greatest potential to change us more into the likeness of Jesus, so that we shine a little brighter, and so, as we go about the rest of the day, there's a little less darkness around.

I don't know if you've ever heard an elite athlete talk about their training routine, but every time I do, I am amazed and challenged at the personal sacrifices people make in order to achieve success. Getting up at 5.00 a.m. every weekday to put in three hours of training before heading to school for a normal day, training again after school and then smashing some homework before going to bed, then doing it all again the next day! We understand that it requires real sacrifice to develop the right muscle groups, techniques and skills to be able to perform at a high level in sport, yet so often we can't imagine making sacrifices anywhere near that level in order that we might grow spiritually strong and skilful.

A few ideas to help you succeed.

1. Do it at the same time every day and in the same place.
2. Start by doing five minutes every day, then gradually build it up as you feel able.
3. Turn off your phone so it can't distract you.
4. Decide about weekends in advance – if you're going to sleep in until 11 a.m., will you still try to make space to meet with Jesus or will you just stick to weekdays?
5. Encourage a friend from church to try doing it too. Share with him or her how you're getting on each week and some of what God has been speaking to you about.

#4

READ THE BIBLE

You probably guessed that this chapter was coming.

A few years ago, I was asked to help out on a school visit to a Jewish synagogue with some students from a school near the church I worked for. I remember the moment that the rabbi showed us where the Torah (effectively the Jewish Bible) was kept. The whole focus of the synagogue was the place in which the Torah was kept – it was called 'The Ark' and was a special cupboard built into the front wall of the synagogue. It was beautifully decorated with a special curtain and, inside, the five scrolls of the Torah had ornate coverings over them. If you wanted to read one, you had to treat it with much reverence and care, as you took the covering off and unrolled the particular part of the scroll you wanted to read, and even as you read it, rather than use your finger to follow the words along, you would use a special silver pointer so that you didn't put dirt or grease from your fingers on the scroll.

I remember this so vividly because, as I sat there watching and listening to the rabbi tell us about this process, I thought to myself that we Christians have somehow forgotten how beautiful and holy our book is (its contents, rather than the pages themselves). I have used mine as a doorstop, left it in various places and even forgotten completely where it is sometimes! I sat there thinking that I needed to start treating my Bible a bit more in line with the value I place on its contents. Before you start to worry, my Bible is still covered in written notes and highlights and sticky notes!

Reading the Bible is one of the things that many of us find hard. We know we should read it, but often we struggle to get into it or even to know where to start or what to read. Once we've gone a while without reading the Bible outside church, we often serve ourselves up a heaped tablespoon of guilt and slump into the (false) belief that 'I must be the worst Christian in history!' Ever been there? I most certainly have.

So let me pass on some helpful thoughts that someone somewhere once passed on to me . . .

Not Just a Book

The Bible is an incredible gift to us. It is God's very word given to us so that we might know him. It is not just a book; it's alive. When we read it, something more happens than words flowing from the page into our minds. Something deeper happens. Something spiritual. Something mysterious. The words reveal a heart and, as we delve into that heart, we are changed. We might not feel different straight away, but we can't help but be affected by a book that is living.

Sometimes we miss the power in what's going on when we read the Bible because, in an intellectual sense, we may not understand fully what we've read. Alternatively, and frankly, reading a list of rules about Old Testament sacrifices in Leviticus isn't massively helpful when you've just split up from your boyfriend or girlfriend (unless you're planning on 'giving him or her to God' in a fairly brutal way!)

Why You Should Read It

We all know we should read it; it's just sometimes hard to remember why. When we know why we are supposed to do something, it helps strengthen our commitment to actually doing it. For example, I love making fires in our firepit and sitting with friends around the glowing embers. I know not to put my hands in the fire. I know WHY I don't put my hands in the fire – because I will get burnt and it will hurt! I know the why and it informs my actions. In the same way, I always put my seatbelt on when I'm driving. Why? Because I know that, first, it's the law and, second, if I have an accident it will be better for everyone if I'm wearing a seatbelt.

So knowing why we should read the Bible is a key part of finding the motivation to actually read it.

Here are five reasons

1. The contents are written for us.
2. The more we read it, the more we'll understand how much God loves us.
3. It's full of truth about who we are.
4. It helps us understand how to love God with our whole lives and shows us where we might be going wrong.
5. It is a light and by it we can see more clearly the path God is leading us on.

How You Read It

There are loads of different ways of reading the Bible. Generally speaking, the hardest way is to just open it up and start reading randomly, but that is actually what so many of us start by doing!

Know a Bit

Knowing a bit about what you're reading can help you work out how to read it or what to read. For example, if you know that you want to read about Jesus, the New Testament is an easier place to start than the Old Testament (although he's in there too!) This will help you narrow down what you're going to read.

Sometimes you might want to know more about a particular subject – for example, worship – so you could do some research to find out if there are any particular books of the Bible that talk specifically about worship. (There's a great passage in Romans 12 if you're interested.)

At other times, reading about someone in the Bible who has experienced similar circumstances or emotions to us can help us navigate how we will respond to what we are going through. For example, the book of Job is about a man called Job who was incredibly blessed, but who then went through the pain of losing much of his family and his possessions. Reading Job's story when we are experiencing pain, loss or grief can give us hope and comfort that others who have lost so much have known God to be with them in the midst of the pain and have held on to their faith.

Just a Bit

When I first started reading the Bible, I began at Genesis 1. I tried to read huge swathes of text in one go and, in the end, I got a bit bored. It was too much for me to take in and to try and find meaning in it.

After a while, I just gave myself small chunks to read – sometimes just a few verses – and I started to enjoy it a lot more. It was less about the quantity I was reading and more about the quality of my attention on these few verses. I found God spoke to me again and again as I would plug away, slowly but deeply, through different books of the Bible.

At some stages in my life I have LOVED the books of Psalms and Proverbs because they are quite easy to break down into small, manageable chunks. These can be great places to go to if you haven't got long to read but want something that packs a punch! Sometimes there will be a line from a psalm or a proverb that is so rich, beautiful or mysterious that it will stay with you all day!

Go a Bit

The slight downside with the last suggestion, 'Just a bit', is that some books of the Bible are really exciting to read in a bigger block. Take, for example, Mark's Gospel: it's fast paced (Mark uses the words 'immediately' or 'straight away' more than 40 times in this book!) and action packed, so it's almost like it was intended to be read in one sitting. When we read parts of the Bible in larger chunks, it can help to give us a much clearer view on the overall subject or the journey of the character.

To help you do this, try to read without stopping at every other sentence to figure out its meaning or ask questions.

Instead, just try to get into 'the flow' of the book and ask God to help you hear what he wants you to, as you read.

SOAP

A few years ago, I heard about something called a 'SOAP Study'. Since then, I have used it hundreds of times to help me read the Bible and apply it to my life. It's incredibly simple and easy!

First, find somewhere to write or take notes. It can be a scrap piece of paper, the back of an old envelope, a journal, anywhere!

Then open up your Bible and read whatever you were planning to read.

Next, write down the letter S (for 'Scripture') and copy a verse or a small chunk from what you have read – something that particularly jumped out at you. It might only be a sentence or a couple of words.

Next, write down the letter O (for 'observation') and make a note of something that it tells you about God, yourself or the character or people involved. What do you notice? What do you find interesting?

Then write the letter A (for 'application'). Now you have to prayerfully consider how you can apply what you've read and observed to your own life. Let's say you have been reading Matthew 14, where Jesus walks on water, then Peter gets out of the boat and walks towards Jesus on the water. Maybe your observation has been something like, 'Peter seems more concerned about being where Jesus is than being safe in the boat.' So now maybe your application might be something like, 'If I feel Jesus prompting me to take some risks today, I'm not going to play it safe – I'm going to step out of the boat towards him.'

The last letter, P (for 'prayer'), is meant to prompt you to write (and pray!) a short prayer, asking the Holy Spirit to help you put into action the application.

Other Ideas

If you really struggle reading the Bible, why not try a different translation from the one you are currently reading? Sometimes it's helpful to try a different translation for a while, even if you find reading your Bible easy!

Also, there are some great audio Bible resources available that are worth checking out. I've included a list of resources at the back, so you've got a place to start. I know a guy in our youth group who managed to listen to the whole of the New Testament while travelling on the bus to and from school. He found it really helpful to listen to it.

#5

RECORD THE STORY

> Hear this, you elders;
> listen, all who live in the land.
> Has anything like this ever happened in your days
> or in the days of your ancestors?
> Tell it to your children,
> and let your children tell it to their children,
> and their children to the next generation.
>
> (Joel 1.2–3)

Before you read those verses and go away thinking that this is a chapter about having children, wait! It isn't! This is a chapter about the art of remembering.

Through the Old Testament, as we read about God's people and the things they lived through (like slavery in Egypt and the ten plagues, the parting of the Red Sea, the years in the wilderness and the eventual crossing of the River Jordan to enter the promised land), there are moments when God reminds his people not to forget what they have seen, heard and experienced. He reminds them to pass on the stories (by word of mouth back in those days) to their children, to retell of the adventure that they, the people of God, have been on and are still living out. God seems to know that if his people don't keep retelling the story, they will forget and, if they forget what God has done in the past, they may also lose sight of what God could do in the future or, in the unseen place, what God might be doing right now in the present that we can't yet see.

The first time my wife, Tabi (back then she was my girlfriend), came to meet my family, I had forgotten just how many photographs of me as a child there were in our family house. They seemed to be everywhere and Tabi took great delight in looking at each one and asking my parents about where it was taken or what I was like as a baby – you know the deal! For each photo, my parents had a story about me as a baby or as a toddler: 'That time he took off his nappy and covered himself in its contents!' 'That time he tried to squeeze through the cat flap.' 'That moment where we reached the summit of the mountain with Bob on his dad's back.' It seemed as though every picture had a story and every story was a little snapshot into who I was and who I have become. Some of the stories were familiar to me, others were new and some I had totally forgotten ever happened.

The people of God didn't have cameras to take snapshots along the journey; all they had were the stories that they told and passed on. Very rarely could anything be written down, so they had to remember. The thing is . . . they often forgot. This is a problem I think I struggle with too (and I'm sure I'm not the only one!) I forget so much of what God has done in my life. The things he's whispered into my heart, the moments he's shown me in a picture or a vision, the words of knowledge he's spoken through people to me or through me to others: so many forgotten moments between the God of the universe and me.

A little while ago, I had a conversation with a young person who was close to walking away from her faith. She was struggling and wanted to talk to me about it. While we were chatting, she said something to me that I will never forget. It was about a time in her early teens when she had encountered God powerfully and felt him speak to her. As she spoke to me, she said, 'I wonder if I just made that up.' I found it difficult to know what to say. I hadn't known her back then or the circumstances of her encounter with God, but my gut was saying that it wouldn't have been like her to make up something like that. I asked her if she had written anything in a journal that she could refer back to and remind herself of more of the details and how she had been feeling at the time. She didn't have any record of it; all that was left of the encounter was an incomplete memory, now with doubts written all over it. I wish she could have looked back at a place where she had written about that moment and been reassured.

Finding somewhere or a way to record our journey with Jesus can be very helpful as we seek to go deeper in our relationship with him. It doesn't have to be a daily outpouring of our soul on to paper (although you might want to do that);

rather, it can be simple notes, jottings, pictures, scribbles, thoughts and feelings, ideas and encouragements, which take no time at all to put down on paper.

I started journaling in my late teens while I was at university and, through the years, I've done it in many different ways and forms. Some of my journals that I have kept are well ordered, with dates and daily entries; others are a bit more all over the place! But they encourage me so deeply as I read over them. Sometimes, as I read stuff in them about what I felt God saying to me or how the message at church had left me pondering, it's like being re-challenged and re-encouraged. I say to myself, 'Wow – I can't believe I had forgotten that truth about Jesus or lost sight of that part of his love for me!'

Some days when I write in my journal, I will write as though I'm talking to God through the page: 'Dear Father, I'm not feeling that positive about this school assembly I am giving today. Please help me not to look like a complete idiot . . . I really need your help and also I heard the neighbours shouting at each other last night. Please just bring your peace into that house, protect their marriage, show me if I can be a blessing to them.'

On other days it will just be a collection of things I've felt God saying to me or things that happened during the day that I want to remember: 'Wow – we just had a time of prophecy at church tonight and someone said that they had a picture of me with huge wings behind me, like angel's wings – wings of protection, not just for me but for others too – that people would come to me for protection. With that a sense of a gift of hospitality.' (That's a real entry from Saturday 13 May, 2012.)

When I look back on things in my journal, I am often stunned at how things have worked out. Even that prophetic word from 2012. As I write this, I look back on how our house has become a home in different seasons to young people who have had to leave their own homes for various reasons and have found safety and refuge living with our family for a while.

With some of the journals I have written in, I have taken them with me almost everywhere. I often carry around a backpack and always have my Bible in there, but having somewhere to write quickly what I think God is saying or something to ponder, has been really helpful. There have been times when I've quickly scribbled in it the prayer request of a young person in the youth group or a team member. At other times, random things will jump out at me as I go about life and I want to remember – a lyric from a song or something that came up in a conversation or a line from a film I was watching. I even remember getting my journal out in a lecture at university. It's true . . . God can even speak through the higher education system.

I say all this because, if your brain is anything like mine, what we don't record we so often forget. Having a record of notes, messages, lines from songs, thoughts and emotions, prayer requests and answers to prayers, things God has whispered to us in the middle of the night or in the middle of a maths lesson, is so encouraging as we look back on these things. They become reminders of God's continual presence with us and of his loving voice that unendingly reaches out to connect with our hearts.

#6

CLEAR THE ROADBLOCK

When I talk to young people about heading back to reality after a period of time away at a summer camp, worship event or festival, I'm often met with a look that I have learned to recognize over the years. It is one that is concerned about a challenge the young person knows he or she will face when landing back in reality.

For some young people, there are challenges that they know they will face to do with circumstances that they can't do anything about. Young people I have worked with through the years have returned to homes where their parents' marriages have been on the rocks or a family member is facing awful health problems or where a carer has lost his or her job and the family is facing crushing financial problems. Many of these kinds of things that we face are issues where all we can do is pray. We can't affect them other than through our prayers. But sometimes we face issues and challenges that we can do something about and, when we decide to, it can help us move forwards in our relationship with Jesus.

Pause for a minute and think about the answer to this question: 'What is one thing or pattern of behaviour that distracts you from your relationship with God?'

Whatever your answer is to that question, wouldn't you love to do something about it? Maybe you are already and, if that's the case, then I applaud you for your courage and willingness to face whatever that giant is. But for those of us who aren't in the fight yet, let me encourage you to get in the ring and land some punches . . .

First Stop: 'Amazing Grace'

The beauty of Jesus' message is that he came for the imperfect and broken people of the world, the people who knew they hadn't got it all together and in their hearts knew that they had fallen short of holiness. Beautiful, isn't it? That Jesus came for those people. It's beautiful to me because I know that I *am* one of those people – imperfect in so many ways, broken and falling short of holiness by a long way.

> Amazing grace, how sweet the sound
> That saved a wretch like me.
> I was once was lost, but now am found
> Was blind but now I see!
>
> (John Newton)

What beautiful news!

But sometimes I realize that, even though this beautiful news is true, some of my thoughts, actions, behaviours and habits hold me back from living as fully connected to God as I really want to be. Ever feel like that?

Second Stop: Walking into Freedom

The stories of normal men and women in the Bible who were used in extraordinary ways by God fill me with hope that, through prayer and action, we can partner with God in finding a greater sense of freedom, fruitfulness and connection to him in our lives. I'm always amazed that God uses superordinary, weak people to partner with and achieve the impossible.

But we have a part to play in 'entering into' all that is available to us in Jesus. Access has been paid for, but to take hold of what is now ours we must move forwards. It's like God has opened a door for us and all we need to do is to walk through it. The people of Israel give us a great picture of what I'm talking about here . . .

God has given them a promise: the promised land, a land flowing with milk and honey (v. nice!) It is to be the place in which they would receive an outpouring of God's blessing. And so the people of Israel go on this journey – beginning with Moses, whom God uses to perform amazing miracles and through whom God eventually loosens Pharaoh's grip around the throat of the people of Israel. The people of Israel witness unbelievable things in this process: plagues of gnats, frogs and darkness and, eventually, the taking of the life of every firstborn male in Egypt. Then, as Pharaoh releases them and they walk out of slavery, a pillar of cloud travels ahead of them in the day and at night . . . God turns on the pyrotechnics – the pillar of cloud turns into a pillar of fire. Imagine seeing all that! Imagine being one of the one million people whom Moses leads out of Egypt. And then it gets even more spectacular! Just when the people of Israel are pinned between the Red Sea and an ensuing army of Egyptian soldiers, God makes a path through the middle of the Red Sea and the people walk through on dry ground. Then, just as the final Israelite reaches safety, the walls of the ocean come crashing down on the Egyptian army, completely destroying them.

Now, that is quite a lot of awesomeness for those people to have witnessed and, just when we think they have seen it all, God starts showering them with bread each morning, so they have something to eat. I mean, seriously, after all that they've seen and collecting bread from heaven each morning, you'd think the people of Israel would have no reason ever to doubt God again. But they do.

When they get to the edge of the promised land, they set up camp and send spies into the land to see how good it is and what they will face when they enter it. The spies come back with a report that the land is amazing – as good as in their dreams – but there are other people living there already and some of them make the spies feel small and weak and fearful when they think about trying to fight them for the land. So the people of Israel hear the report from the spies and they tremble in fear, exclaiming that they could never face the giants in the promised land and that they are simply not strong enough to take hold of the amazing country that has been promised to them by God. The Israelites then turn around and walk away from the land flowing with milk and honey – and they walk around in circles in the desert for 40 years!

Sometimes when we look at the people of Israel we can see a little bit of ourselves. Fear and concern can sometimes hold us back from taking hold of some of God's promises for our own lives. Often those fears or concerns can be linked to the giants that we might have to face if we are going to set foot in the promised land. We look at the size of the challenge and what it could cost us – time, energy, friendships, grades, status or significance – and we walk away, unwilling or unable to fathom the cost.

I have done this countless times. I know I have been set free from being a slave to sin (Jesus has paid for my freedom with his sacrifice) and that I am on an incredible adventure with Jesus, walking more and more fully into the promises he has for me. Yet, to enter into those promises, I must sometimes face a giant and, if I don't, I often feel a bit like I'm going round and round in circles in the desert when it comes to my walk with Jesus.

OK, so let me throw a few ideas at you to get you thinking more about what your roadblocks might be . . .

Comfort

We don't want to change or we can't really be bothered to change or it's too much like hard work to change. I know in my own life that reaching for the comfortable life is one of the biggest roadblocks that stops me growing and it distracts me from my relationship with God. I am scared of uncertainty and it holds me back.

Image (Real and Online)

We all want to look good, don't we? As far as I can tell, there's nothing wrong with that to a certain extent, but when it becomes something that we focus on and get obsessive about, it can start to derail our relationships with others and with God. We can start to believe the lie that we are not good enough unless we look a certain way, wear a particular brand or fit into a certain size category.

Pornography

Standing up to the giant of porn can seem daunting, especially if you're regularly viewing it and maybe caught up in a bit of an addiction to it. This giant also seems to counteract any sign of attack by unleashing on you a barrel-load of shame, should you even think about trying to defeat it. In the last ten years, I have met young people from all over the world who are struggling with porn and wanting help. So many of them find that they feel distant from God because of their attachment to porn and the guilt that comes from watching it. There are tons of places you can go to help you find some practical tools to begin fighting back against pornography (I've listed some at the back of the book).

Relationships

Relationships are some of the best gifts that God gives to us. They can be life-giving, encouraging, safe-to-be-vulnerable places that bring a richness and depth to life. However, if our lives become centred on having a boyfriend or a girlfriend, we end up investing so much more time, energy and emotion in the relationship we either want or have than we do in our relationship with God.

Sex

God invented sex. He thinks it's great. He made it an incredibly powerful act of intimacy. He also designed an incredibly powerful relationship to house the power of sex, so that its beauty be fully enjoyed. That relationship is called marriage.

Becoming sexual with a boyfriend or girlfriend is going to get in the way of your relationship with God. It's as plain and simple as that. The difficulty is that it's natural for your body to want your romantic relationships to become sexual in some way. Your body is wired that way and it's a fierce battle to hold on to your hormones!

God, in his amazing grace, has forgiven and will forgive every mistake we make in this area, but there is so much we can do to be wise ahead of time and find ways to honour God and each other in romantic relationships.

Money

Jesus talks loads about money in the New Testament. He is aware that money is powerful and it can corrupt and distract anyone. We live in a world that is obsessed by it and celebrates those who have accumulated it. Is your life geared towards making money so that you can do x, y or z? Jesus reminds us, 'But seek first his kingdom and his righteousness, and all these things will be given to you as well' (Matthew 6.33).

Your Phone

You see that little thing over there that provides endless connection and entertainment? Well, if I'm honest, mine distracts me quite a bit from being with Jesus. I'm not suggesting you fling it out of the window, but what about having a set time in the day where you put it away? Maybe you put it away for 15 minutes and spend some time with God or maybe you put it away for a few hours and just enjoy being without it?

#7

GO AFTER THE KINGDOM TODAY

Jesus said:

> **'But seek first his kingdom and his righteousness, and all these things will be given to you as well.'** (Matthew 6.33)

Trying to live in the fullness of this promise is exciting. When we do it, it's like suddenly reading life the way a computer coding genius looks at code – most people are utterly confused by it, but the coder knows what it all means.

We've said before that the Christian faith is all about a relationship with Jesus Christ. Nothing makes sense unless we start there. But as we move on from that point, we soon realize that this relationship begins to affect the way we walk and talk and see the world around us. The presence of God in our lives through the Holy Spirit makes us a living, breathing dynamo of infinite potential, filled with his power and love. We may not always feel like it, but that is the truth.

Seeking the kingdom of God means looking for, searching for, having an awareness for moments when we can be a part of a situation that reveals God's heart. It's having a readiness to say, 'If I go and do something in that situation, we could see more of God's heart.'

Let me give you an example . . .

Imagine you're sitting in the school canteen with your friends, having a great conversation, laughing and joking. Suddenly you notice that slightly strange character from your form on her own, sitting and eating by herself. She looks lonely. As you watch, she's approached by a group of girls from the year below and they throw a few insults at her. You watch as she takes their insults in and they seem to pull her lower into the chair. Already disengaged from whatever your friends are talking about now, you slide out of your chair and move towards her without saying anything to anyone. You draw up alongside her, you look her in the eye and ask to sit there, in the chair next to her, and finish your lunch with her. You don't really know what to say, but at least she's not on her own any more.

That is seeking the kingdom of God in a school canteen.

What we read about heaven in the Bible (actually, surprisingly little!) tells us more of what the kingdom of God is like. One of the things we begin to understand about heaven is that there is complete restoration of relationships: with God, with one another and with the world. One of the implications of our relationships with one another being utterly and wonderfully perfected is that loneliness will be eradicated. Think about that for a second: there aren't any lonely people in heaven. So, getting back to my example above, when you move in on a situation in your school canteen to make sure that the lonely person isn't on their own any more, you have sought out the kingdom of God. At that moment when you did what you did, fuelled by the love and power of God within you, you opened the door for heaven to come down.

A few months ago, we were talking about the kingdom of God in our youth group. We were looking at it from the perspective of what the kingdom of God is like – different characteristics of the kingdom. One evening we were talking about how one of God's characteristics is that he's not stingy – he's incredibly generous – and so part of us 'seeking the kingdom of God' was about looking for opportunities every day to be generous. At the end of the evening, we gave everyone a 50-pence piece, along with the challenge to 'go and bring the kingdom with this at some stage in the next week and bring back the story when we next have youth group'. Now 50p isn't a massively generous sum, but it wasn't meant to be: it was meant to be the stimulus for each of us to be generous, like carrying around in our pocket a generosity reminder.

There were loads of stories that came back the following week. We shared them with each other and, as I listened, I was absolutely inspired by each of the young people.

One of my favourite stories was from a guy called Dylan, who was 15 at the time. He took his 50p and added some of his own money so that he could buy a coffee for a homeless man he had seen sitting against a wall in the town centre. Dylan got the man a coffee, then sat with him for almost an hour, talking with him, asking him about his life and listening to him talk about all that he had been through. Then Dylan asked if he could pray with the man and the man said, 'Yes.'

That is seeking the kingdom of God on the high street.

Sometimes we won't even recognize these moments straight away as 'seeking first the kingdom', but later we'll understand how they reflected something of the heart and character of God. The kingdom of God is, after all, a reflection of the heart of its king. We followers of Jesus are often so fixated on seeing some spectacular healing or miracle that we can miss some of the most beautiful, quiet, gentle opportunities for us to be part of bringing heaven to earth.

Seeing people's limbs grow back, vertebrae realign, sight being restored or cancerous cells disappear is the kingdom of God. I deeply and passionately long to see more of those miracles, both in our churches and outside, but we must not miss the fact that love can be expressed in both the healing and the holding of broken people.

A few years ago, I took a group of young people to Uganda in Africa. One afternoon we were praying for people on the street and a lady came to us who was deaf in one ear. We asked her which ear it was and then my friend Zoe and I put our hands on the ear and prayed really simply that she be healed in Jesus' name. After a while of what seemed like nothing happening, she opened her eyes and grinned at us and then tried to explain with gestures and hand signals that she could hear again! Zoe and I were a little shocked, to be honest! That was the kingdom of God.

When I reflect on that trip, though, the thing I will always remember most fondly is the way that the young people revealed what the kingdom of God is like to the man who drove our bus around for the two weeks we were there.

His name was Yokolam and the young people made him feel like he was the best thing since sliced bread. They got to know him, learned his name, sang about him, shared their food with him, learned about his children, his wife, his upbringing, where he lived and so much more. They made Yokolam feel like he was worth getting to know, that he was valuable, memorable and important to them and to what we were doing. They made sure he was included, not forgotten or cast aside. These are things that are in God's heart for Yokolam. God's heart longs for Yokolam to know that he's worth getting to know, that he's valuable, unforgettable, important to God's plans on this earth. Maybe heaven resounds with these truths and those young people brought a little bit of heaven to earth for Yokolam over those two weeks.

The challenge Jesus gives us is to 'seek first his kingdom' and, when he teaches his disciples how to pray, he tells them to say, 'Your kingdom come, your will be done' (Matthew 6.10). As we desire to grow closer to Jesus, our hearts will align more and more with his, and our longing to see the kingdom of God will become a greater passion as we live each day, and in how we pray.

Just to help ground this, why not try a couple of these suggestions.

1. Begin to pray about the kingdom of God and ask God to show you opportunities where you can be involved.
2. Talk with a Christian friend about something you see in the world around you (in your home/street/town/school/college/university/city/nation) that upsets you or is wrong or just seems a million miles away from the way God intended it to be. Ask the question, 'How could we bring the kingdom of God into that situation?'
3. Have a go.

#8 FIND A WAY TO TELL YOUR MATES YOU'RE A CHRISTIAN

(*AND* WHAT A DIFFERENCE IT'S MADE TO YOU TO BE IN RELATIONSHIP WITH HIM)

There's a story in Luke 5 that tells of the time Jesus called some of the first disciples. As we read it, we find that Jesus is standing on the shore of a huge lake called the Sea of Galilee. People are flocking around him, desperate to hear what he is saying and teaching. In the end, the crowd must have grown to a size that is difficult for him to speak to. Jesus spots an opportunity:

> **He saw at the water's edge two boats, left there by the fishermen, who were washing their nets. He got into one of the boats, the one belonging to Simon [Peter], and asked him to put out a little from shore. Then he sat down and taught the people from the boat. (Luke 5.2–3)**

Jesus knows it will be easier to teach the people if he's in a boat, a little way out from the shore, so that he can address his audience all at once, rather than trying to make sure everyone can hear as they crowd around him on all sides. But while this moment shows how Jesus is into practical solutions to problems, something bigger is going on. Peter has been faced with a request from Jesus: basically, 'Can I use your boat?' Peter's response changes the rest of his entire life. We don't know if Peter replied with a verbal, 'Yes you can, Jesus', or whether he just did as Jesus asked, but whatever he did, it implied that he was giving his permission for Jesus to step into his boat and to use it for whatever Jesus had planned.

The thing I often reflect on in that story is the boat is where Peter spends his everyday life. It is his school classroom or his work office or his factory floor. It is where he lives his normal, everyday life and, in this moment, he allows Jesus to step into it. He gives Jesus a place and permission in his everyday, normal life.

Romans 12 in *The Message* calls on followers of Jesus to give him their everyday normal life . . . to let Jesus into your boat.

> **Place Your Life Before God**
>
> **So here's what I want you to do, God helping you: Take your everyday, ordinary life – your sleeping, eating, going-to-work, and walking-around life – and place it before God as an offering. (Romans 12.1–2)**

With Jesus in your boat, something will undoubtedly begin to happen, as it does in the story from Luke. Jesus will begin to speak to people around you about who he is and about his kingdom. It may not always happen with words, but with your boat surrendered to Jesus, you can be sure that he will want to use it to reveal the truth of who he is to the world around you.

I remember the first time I really felt Jesus asking if he could step into my boat and speak to people in my world through me. I was in a sex education lesson at school and I was about 14.

I had been a Christian since the age of about nine or ten and loved being a part of church and the youth group that we had. My walk with Jesus was definitely growing. It was nowhere near perfect, but it was moving forwards. School, though, was the one place where I really didn't want God to show up. My friends had an idea of what Christianity was and they didn't seem to like it. I was fearful about people finding out that I was different from them, that I believed in something that I didn't have all the answers for and couldn't prove the reality of. Most of all, I was scared of being different, of standing out from the crowd, so I kept my head down, got on with school and tried to push Jesus out of my boat whenever it felt like he was wanting to step into it.

So there I was, 14 years old, running into the maths classroom after break-time. I was late because we'd been having some sort of penalty shoot-out that had gone to sudden death! Believe me . . . it was as important as a World Cup Final. So I arrived in the classroom last and the only seat left was right in front of the teacher's desk. I made my way forwards, flopped into the chair, adrenaline still pumping, slid my bag off my back on to the floor and grabbed my pencil case. As I adjusted in my seat, I saw right in front of me on the teacher's desk some things that I had never seen before. I knew very well what they were (an array of condoms, leaflets with half-naked people on the front, etc), but I hadn't ever seen them and I began to feel the temperature of my cheeks going through the roof. Not the lesson that a very sheltered, prudish young lad from a leafy suburb of London wants to be sitting in the front row for.

Our teacher, a man called Mr Wilson, seemed to spring up from behind the desk like a jack-in-the-box, dressed in a suit, with big round glasses and a mop of curly hair. He very excitedly introduced the theme and proceeded through the lesson, with 14-year-old Bob Wallington sinking further and further into the seat in front of him and turning an even brighter shade of embarrassed!

The moment came, though, in this particular lesson about sex, when Mr Wilson began to ask the class some questions (after the obligatory putting-a-condom-on-a-banana routine was over and done with). I don't remember any of the questions that he asked, other than this one: 'The legal age for a consensual sexual relationship in the UK is 16. Who here thinks that at the age of 16 you'll be ready for a sexual relationship?'

Hold. The. Phone.

Before I could think, I could see, out of the corner of my eye, my friends lifting their hands so quickly that it seemed they were responding to a question like, 'Who wants a million pounds?!' Within seconds, everyone I could see had their hand practically through the roof. And there I was, feeling like the question I was being asked was entirely different: 'Can I get into your boat, Bob?'

At our youth group we had spoken about God's intention for sex to be within the context of marriage. I had decided then and there that I wanted to follow that plan, to wait, however hard that might be, until I was married before having sex.

And now here I was, in a class of people that I didn't want to be different from or stand out among, faced with this question. I remember gripping the sides of my chair and praying very simply that I was 'all in'. No longer did I want to live two different lives. I was going to let Jesus into my boat.

So I kept my hands down, away from any light fittings or ceiling panels. Then the most amazing thing happened: Mr Wilson moved on and asked another question. People started responding to it. My response had gone unnoticed. 'Thank you, God!' I thought, until a voice from the back interrupted Mr Wilson and politely asked why I didn't think I'd be ready for a sexual relationship when I was 16?

It was at this point that I began praying for an earthquake, a volcanic eruption or even the second coming of Jesus, so that I wouldn't have to answer the question. But none came. I turned around to my classmates and tried to explain that

I was a Christian and my understanding was, God's design for sex was that it should take place within marriage and I didn't expect to be married when I was 16 years old and therefore wouldn't be ready for a sexual relationship.

There was silence.

The lesson ended. The day moved on and I was faced with a barrage of questions from my friends. Most of the questions involved some kind of scenario where an incredibly beautiful girl walks naked into my bedroom and begs me for sex. 'What would you do then, huh??' they asked. But after a while came questions about my faith. What do you believe? What's your church like? Is being a Christian all about rules that mean you don't have fun? Can I come to your church?

I look back on this moment in that classroom as the moment I let Jesus into my boat and, since that moment, my life hasn't been the same.

Finding ways to tell our friends and family about Jesus is one of the best ways of growing in our faith. It will challenge us, stretch us and present us with questions that we may not have heard answers to before. But it will also grow our trust in Jesus as we share about him with others. I have often found that, in these moments, my friends don't necessarily want to know what I believe; they want to know what difference it has made in my life – they are kind of asking. 'Is the "good news" really good news?'

> **'But in your hearts revere Christ as Lord. Always be prepared to give an answer to everyone who asks you to give the reason for the hope that you have. But do this with gentleness and respect.' (1 Peter 3.15)**

This verse from 1 Peter is a great inspiration to me, but in my younger years it always used to worry me. I wasn't sure if I would be able to answer coherently and confidently when people asked me about my faith or if I knew enough theology to answer their questions. One of my greatest fears was of being outsmarted by a militant atheist in front of a group of my friends and then, because of my answer (or lack of it), those friends would move further away from coming to know Jesus rather than closer to him. Thankfully, this hasn't ever happened to me, but there have been plenty of times when I haven't been able to answer people's questions about Jesus or the way the Bible teaches us to live. Through the years I have become more at peace in these situations because the following two things are true.

1. God is mysterious and not everything can be, or has to be, explained in order for it to be truth.
2. God is the one who works in people's hearts, not me. When faced with a question I don't know the answer to, I'll

honestly say, 'I don't know.' Then I will either try to find an answer from someone with a bit more theology knowledge than me or just pray that God would work in the heart of that person and show them that he is there.

I know many of us share my concerns that we don't know enough to answer people's questions, but I'm always amazed at how good new believers are at telling other people about Jesus, in spite of their lack of experience as Christians. As people who have just become Christians talk to others about Jesus, they don't very often focus on the vast intellectual and theological questions and answers. Instead, they focus on the amazing grace that they have experienced or the father heart of God that has enveloped them in a love that they have never experienced before or the forgiveness that Jesus' sacrifice on the cross made possible and the liberty and freedom they now know in their life because of it.

When we talk to our friends about Jesus and what difference he has made in our lives, it's serving two purposes:

1. our friends get to hear about the Good News of Jesus Christ and the love that God has for them;
2. we are reminded of what is at the core of our faith, the foundation of our relationship with God and how we have been able to know his great love for us.

#9

REFUSE TO MOAN ABOUT THE CHURCH

Churches can be funny things! I mean, think about it . . . they're basically collections of people, all of whom are imperfect, have differing opinions, tastes, likes, dislikes and values, along with varying levels of brokenness. These people then come together to form a community. The reality is going to be (at least at times) far from our dreams.

So what do we human beings do when the thing we are involved in is less than we dreamed it would be? We moan and complain. We chew people's ears off about how we'd do it differently if we could and how much better our (in this case, church) would be if we were to change this or that particular aspect.

For some of us it will be that we don't like the building we meet in or the songs we sing or the format the service takes or the person doing the preaching or the way we welcome people. Everyone who is part of a church community will be able to point to something they would like to see done differently. There are no perfect churches.

The thing is, most of us aren't expecting church to be perfect; we just want it to be better. Somewhere in this longing to see church services and communities operating more effectively is a good and noble desire that we would be the best we can be. As long as it doesn't become a striving for perfectionism, that desire can be used to move our church more into the shape and purposes that God has for it. But we must move with great care and honour as we seek to help our church to move forwards. We must, with all our hearts, try to resist the temptation to moan, complain and point fingers at the parts of our church that we see as being imperfect.

Let me illustrate why, by painting a picture of my wedding day. There I was, in my navy-blue suit at the front of the church, flanked by my brothers, awaiting the arrival of my bride, Tabi. Nothing prepares you for the moment when, arm in arm with her father, the woman you want to spend the rest of your life with walks slowly, gracefully and purposefully down the aisle to meet you. In that moment, as Tabi walked towards me, I was utterly overwhelmed. She was perfect. Beautiful. Radiant and shining as she made her way towards me. The emotions set in. I was delirious with joy. My lip started to quiver. A millisecond before I turned into a blubbering mess on the floor, she arrived, took my hand, looked into my eyes and grinned. I promise you, if that aisle had been a metre longer and she had taken a second longer to reach me, I would have lost it!

Now, imagine for a moment that, as Tabi stood there on our wedding day at the entrance to the church, some people from within the church had started to name out loud things that weren't to their taste about Tabi or her dress or the flowers she was holding. I would have been devastated and Tabi would have felt awful. No doubt we would have gone over to those people and politely punched them in the face. Tabi and I are both imperfect people and we are both aware of that fact. When Tabi was standing at the front of the church in her beautiful white dress, she was not saying to the world, 'I'm perfect!' She wasn't walking towards me trying to convince me that she was utterly perfect in every way either. In that moment, though, there wasn't a single trace of a thought going through my mind that was raising awareness of any of Tabi's imperfections. I was in awe, in love with her, and that love was powerful enough for me to overlook every imperfection. To me she was perfect. She would say the same about me, that her love for me was enough to enable her to see me perfectly, even though she knew I wasn't (and am still far from) perfect.

When we moan and complain about our church, it's like we are finding imperfections in a bride waiting to be joined to her husband.

The Church is referred to in the Bible as the bride of Christ. Jesus loves the Church like I love Tabi, but with a perfect, pure, unending love. Jesus is crazy about the Church! He can see past all its imperfections because of his great love for it.

To some of us, this may seem slightly out of place in a list of practical ways to take our relationship with Jesus to a deeper level. Does it really matter what I say about my church in private or what I think about the Church in my heart? Well, yes, it does. How we approach the imperfection of the church we are part of will have a bearing on our spiritual growth and our relationship with Jesus.

It goes without saying that, if somehow the church you are a part of has got to the point where its dysfunction or imperfection is actually causing harm to your well-being, then you ought to seek advice and take steps to make yourself safe (which might include leaving that church, if need be). Most of us, thankfully, will only be faced with issues of imperfection and dysfunction that leave us a bit annoyed, disappointed or sometimes a bit bored. In these times we need to hold on to three characteristics of Jesus:

Forgiveness

You will need to forgive your church, and the people who are part of it, many times. Human beings have a tendency to let each other down and make mistakes. The Church does not profess to be a collection of perfect people and so imperfection will inevitably lead to the need for forgiveness. We, I am sure, will also need forgiveness from others in our church when we mess up.

Commitment

Jesus was totally committed to the 12 disciples and a wider group of followers. They were his church and (apart from him) they were all imperfect, yet Jesus was totally committed to them. He didn't walk away and leave them when they misunderstood him or got things wrong. He didn't eject them from the group when they couldn't do what he said. He loved them, despite all their failings and shortcomings, and was committed to them.

Self-giving Sacrifice

We see this best displayed on the cross when Jesus lay down his life for the entirety of humankind, not just those who believed in him in that moment. He made a way for everyone who would acknowledge him as God to be reunited with God. He gave himself up so that we might experience relationship with God. Following that example, we too must make sacrifices. Maybe that involves giving up some time to serve somewhere in your church (there's a chapter on that later!) or being less concerned with the way you want it to be and a little more open to other people's thoughts and ideas.

> **'Husbands, love your wives, just as Christ loved the church and gave himself up for her.' (Ephesians 5.25)**

It becomes increasingly difficult to slag something off when you have decided in your heart that you will forgive it, that you're totally committed to it and you are willing to sacrifice big parts of your life to see it flourish and grow.

When we've chosen in our hearts not to speak badly about our church, we basically have no option but to speak well of it. We're forced to find things about the church that we can talk positively about.

Proverbs 18.21 says that 'the tongue has the power of life and death' and, as I speak about my church, I want to make sure that I am speaking life over it, not death.

This is much easier on paper than it is in reality, but that doesn't mean it's not worth your energy and effort. As you begin to see your church the way Jesus sees it and to love it more and more like he loves it, you will know more of his heart living in yours, and this won't just affect the way you see your church.

#10

LEARN TO FEED YOURSELF

As a youth pastor, there are a few things that make me whoop and shout and fist-pump the nearest person. One of those things is when I discover that young people in my youth group are actively seeking ways to grow in their relationship with Jesus outside church or youth group and all without me making any suggestions. This might take the form of them working through some Bible study notes or videos they've found or a book they're reading about something to do with faith or the latest worship playlist that is on non-stop repeat on their Spotify account or just simply that they're reading the Bible in their own time and loving it.

Why, you may ask, is that something which makes me, and other youth pastors around the globe, do a little dance, whoop and fist-pump random strangers?! Well, it's because it signals a shift in who those young people think is responsible for their relationship with Jesus.

It's very easy to assume that the responsibility for your relationship with God lies with the church you attend or the pastor you see most regularly or the leaders of your cell/connect/community group. But that simply isn't the case. The leaders of the church obviously want to do their jobs well and to take seriously the responsibility that God has given them, but they cannot be responsible for every individual's relationship with Jesus. That is up to each of us to own.

Think about that for a moment. If the church leaders are the only ones responsible for you growing in your relationship with God, then realistically you're very limited in how and when your spiritual life can develop.

When I was in my teenage years, I would often get home from school and be absolutely starving. I didn't know much about cooking, but my parents taught me how to cook a few easy (and delicious) snacks/meals that I could rustle up in an emergency (pretty much every day). I was a pro at French toast; I could make, bake and eat an apple crumble in less than an hour; and I was even able to rustle up a delicious cottage pie! As time went on, I added to my recipe list and, by the time I left home for university, I wasn't worried at all about whether or not I could survive by cooking my own meals.

What we're looking at here isn't too dissimilar to my first ventures into cooking. Had I never learnt to cook those snacks and meals, I would have been totally reliant on my parents to provide my food. I would have needed to wait until they were home from work and had the time to cook before I could eat and receive the sustenance I was craving. Moving away from home to university would also have been a huge challenge without the necessary kitchen know-how.

So why the celebration when people take responsibility for their own relationship with Jesus? Because owning that responsibility, rather than assuming it is someone else's, means that you can begin to really mature and grow as a follower of Jesus. Your growth and depth of relationship with Jesus is no longer linked directly only to what happens on a Sunday in church, but to what happens on the other six days of the week. Your walk with Jesus doesn't grind to a halt if you're ill or away for the weekend and have to miss church, because you're feeding your soul and investing in your relationship with Jesus during the week.

I was chatting recently to a friend of mine who is an amazing youth pastor. During the conversation we somehow got talking about a group of lads in her youth group who were 16, 17 and 18 years old. They had started getting together every now and then (without any involvement from their leaders) to hang out, read the Bible together (one of them would share afterwards what they thought God was saying), pray together and then later play ridiculous games in the dark! She was so encouraged by what they were doing and I was too.

Over the years I have found so many different places from which I can learn, grow and see my relationship with God deepen. Sometimes it is unexpected, like an album that I have started to listen to that really got me thinking or inspired me about a certain aspect of my faith. At other times I have more intentionally wanted to spend some time investing in my relationship with God and have tried to spend a chunk of time studying the Bible or reading a particular book that I knew would help deepen my understanding of God.

Here are some ideas that might help you:

- Bible study notes
- Bible in One Year app
- Bible in One Year (youth-specific)
- *God's Smuggler* by Brother Andrew (Hodder & Stoughton, 2008)
- *Run Baby Run* by Nicky Cruz (Hodder & Stoughton, 2003)
- *Chasing the Dragon* by Jackie Pullinger (Hodder & Stoughton, 2006).

#11

DON'T BE SO DEPENDENT ON 'FEELING IT'

In my late teenage years, the church I was part of started a new, incredibly exciting camp for 11- to 14-year-olds. Our church was joining with three other churches to combine resources and ideas in order that we could put on an amazing few days away.

I was really excited when my youth pastor, Andy, asked if I would come to the camp as a leader and help make it all happen. Of course, I said, 'Yes!' I ended up as a leader on the camp for the following four or five summers. Each year seemed to get better and better and I just didn't want to miss it. The best part of it all was hearing how the young people were meeting Jesus. As we met together in the mornings and evenings, the young people were encountering the love of God in tangible ways as the Holy Spirit filled them, healed them, equipped them and inspired them. It was electric, exciting, absolutely wonderful!

Some of the young people, as they met with God, had experiences where they really sensed the presence of God on them or inside them. For some of them it was a beautiful sense of peace and comfort that suddenly filled them, despite awful situations they faced in their lives. For others it was a more dynamic sense of power that they experienced – it made their hearts beat noticeably faster or they had a sense of heat in their body or just a great sense of excitement and enthusiasm that seemed to be bubbling up from the inside.

Other young people (and leaders) met with Jesus too and were filled with his Holy Spirit, but didn't really feel anything at all.

Years later, I happened to meet some of the young people who had been on those camps and met with Jesus in tangible ways – they had physically felt the presence of God in one way or another. One of them spoke with me for a long time about his journey of faith since we had last seen each other at camp. Sadly, he explained to me that he had almost lost all belief in God. It was heartbreaking to hear some of his story and the things that had left him questioning the existence of God. Most painfully of all, he began to tell me about a time when he had thought he was encountering the Holy Spirit at camp and how real it had been to him in that moment, but now, years later, as he looked back, he was worried that he had made it all up. While trying to reassure him, I heard him say something that really stood out to me, something that I have heard many times since from other young people: 'I just can't feel God the way that I did back then . . .'

For some young people, the 'back then' part of that statement can mean 'a few weeks ago'; for others it's talking about a longer period of time, but there are many, many followers of Jesus who can relate to this feeling. If this is true for you, fear not!

One of the most frustrating things about God is that he's mysterious. He can't be understood like the engine of a car or be fully perceived by our incredible, but tiny, human brains. All the mystery and awe of God means that we don't know why sometimes God's presence engages our senses and at other times does not. We can't answer definitively why at church I might know the Holy Spirit's presence in my body, quickening my heart or lavishing me with waves of his love one week, and the next, I don't feel anything at all. The truth that we must hold on to is that God can meet with his people in ways that they can sense or feel and in ways that they might not. Just because someone does not physically feel or sense the presence of God doesn't mean that he has not met with them.

Jesus promised his disciples that, 'where two or three gather in my name, there am I with them' (Matthew 18.20). So Jesus promises us that his presence is with us, by the Holy Spirit, whenever we gather in his name.

King David wrote a psalm that might be familiar to many of us. In the middle of it he writes about the presence of God:

> Where can I go from your Spirit?
> Where can I flee from your presence?
> If I go up to the heavens, you are there;
> if I make my bed in the depths, you are there.
> If I rise on the wings of the dawn,
> if I settle on the far side of the sea,
> even there your hand will guide me,

your right hand will hold me fast.
If I say, 'Surely the darkness will hide me
and the light become night around me,'
even the darkness will not be dark to you;
the night will shine like the day,
for darkness is as light to you.

(Psalm 139.7–12)

He's basically saying that there's nowhere he could go and not be in the presence of God! Isn't that an amazing thought, that God's presence is everywhere? His presence is in your maths classroom at school and on your bus home; it's filling your bedroom, your bathroom, your garage and your garden.

Jeremiah 23.24 says:

'Who can hide in secret places
so that I cannot see them?'
declares the LORD.
'Do not I fill heaven and earth?'
declares the LORD.

So God is everywhere, all the time, filling up the entire universe with his presence and, in addition to that, he's underlined that he's definitely there when two or three (or more!) of his children meet together. So if that is the case, even though we might not physically 'experience' God's presence, we can be sure that it's there.

What's difficult to answer is why sometimes we experience the Holy Spirit in tangible ways and sometimes we don't. But even when we don't 'feel' the presence of God, he is, by his very nature, as present with us as he ever has been.

So when we worry that God has left us or if he ever even existed, all because we haven't 'experienced' him recently when we've asked to be filled with the Holy Spirit, it's actually a sign that our thinking needs reshaping.

Another thing that would be good to remember in these moments of doubt or concern that we aren't receiving the Holy Spirit, because we aren't feeling anything different, is that God is by his very nature good. He reveals himself in the Bible as a loving, caring, good Father – so much so, that he wants us to call him, and see him as, 'Daddy'.

Jesus reminds his disciples that they know how to give good gifts to their children and their heavenly Father is infinitely better, more loving and good, than any human father could ever be (Matthew 7.11).

God's desire is that you be filled with the fullness of his Spirit, that you might know him and his great love for you and that you might be filled with that love in order to be his witness on the earth.

Matthew 7.7–8 says:

> **'Ask and it will be given to you; seek and you will find; knock and the door will be opened to you. For everyone who asks receives; the one who seeks finds; and to the one who knocks, the door will be opened.'**

In a world that demands proof and concrete evidence for almost everything, it can be easy to wire our thinking that way when it comes to matters of spirituality. The truth is that receiving and being filled with the Holy Spirit requires faith. It's not that we have to do something special in order to receive the Holy Spirit: all we have to do is believe that God wants to fill us with his Spirit and that when we ask, he will do exactly that.

The writer of Hebrews says that 'faith is confidence in what we hope for and assurance about what we do not see' (Hebrews 11.1). If we apply this to being filled with the Holy Spirit, then faith is confidence in being filled with the Spirit and assurance that God is pouring his Holy Spirit into us, even if we aren't feeling any different or showing any outward sign of what is happening.

If you were ever to visit our church in Watford, you'd notice that at some stage in every service we try to give people an opportunity to receive prayer, so that the Holy Spirit can fill them and help them, heal them, set them free, empower them, envision them or – best of all – simply fill them with his love.

Sometimes when I pray for people, it seems like nothing is happening, but afterwards, when I ask them, they have often met with God in amazing and deep ways. At other times I might pray for someone and I can visibly see that the Holy Spirit is working in them. It might be that they suddenly look incredibly peaceful or, if there's pain that God is healing, they may begin to cry or sometimes people might shake slightly or even want to lie down. Whatever is happening, whether it's visible or not, or whether the person we're praying for feels any different or not, by faith we believe that God is at work, pouring his great love into our hearts, as the best dad in the world would want to do for his kids.

#12

START TO SERVE

One of the things about following Jesus is that some of the things he said and ways he called us to live (so we might reflect his heart to the world around us) require us to go against some of our most natural inclinations. By that I mean Jesus said we should do some things that essentially look like hard, grubby work, which most of us would rather not do, especially when life has presented us with the alternative option of watching Netflix. The most obvious of these is the call to give up our lives in order that we might truly find life: to take up our cross and follow him (Matthew 16.24).

Serving our church is another of those 'not really what I feel like doing 'things that Jesus calls each of us to. He modelled it to us throughout his ministry, but especially in a major moment just before he was to be arrested. He was eating the Passover meal with his disciples (his community), when he suddenly seemed to have some kind of identity crisis and took a towel, wrapped it around his waist and began to wash the disciples' feet.

This was the job of a servant, not of the God of the universe in human form. It wasn't just the job of *any* servant either; it was the job of the least-important servant, the lowest servant on the rung. The reason it was the job of the least-important servant is that it was the worst job! Back in those days they didn't wear covered shoes like we do today; they wore sandals. 'Fine,' you might say, 'I don't mind sandals', until you take into account that they didn't have any underground sewage systems. Instead, they had overground sewage systems, and by that I mean the disciples would have been walking through a good amount of human waste whenever they entered a large town or city. Jesus waited until they were in the major city of Jerusalem to pull this stunt. But it's not a stunt. It's a message with a very clear implication.

> When he had finished washing their feet, he put on his clothes and returned to his place. 'Do you understand what I have done for you?' he asked them. 'You call me "Teacher" and "Lord", and rightly so, for that is what I am. Now that I, your Lord and Teacher, have washed your feet, you also should wash one another's feet. I have set you an example that you should do as I have done for you. Very truly I tell you, no servant is greater than his master, nor is a messenger greater than the one who sent him. Now that you know these things, you will be blessed if you do them.' (John 13.12–17)

Jesus says to the guys who are going to be the ones who form the first-ever church, 'I have set you an example that you should do as I have done for you.' This example is to be a part of the very fibre of the Church of Jesus: people willing to metaphorically wash each other's feet; leaders not esteemed and put on pedestals, but whose hands and hearts are found serving in the places no one else wants to.

This is a defining characteristic of the Church and one that is not just for some people to engage in, but for every part and member to find a way to join in with. One of the reasons it's so important is that serving one another is one of the fundamental ways in which we show love to one another and love is *the* defining characteristic of the Church. In order to show love to one another, we must serve one another and to serve one another requires us to sacrifice of our own needs/time/desires/comfort in order that others around us would flourish. This is a picture of the cross, lived out by each of us.

This might take the form of a role that you sign up to do regularly in order to serve your church, such as setting out the chairs or helping in the kids' programme or serving the teas and coffees. But it could also be a readiness to help out when something needs doing.

Later, after Jesus had washed his disciples' feet, he explained to them:

> **'By this everyone will know that you are my disciples, if you love one another.'** (John 13.35)

We often forget, or don't realize, that one of the core strategies Jesus gave us for seeing people come into relationship with him is for those in the Church to love one another well, make sacrifice for one another and serve one another.

When I was growing up, I used to hear people say that my friends and I were 'the Church of the future'. I liked the idea that one day I would get to be part of the real thing. But at some point I remember someone challenging the statement and calling each of us, as young people, to realize that we were part of the church NOW. It wasn't some mystical thing that would suddenly happen in the future when we were adults, but we were a crucial, important, wonderful part of the church now.

And so, with that knowledge, let's not wait a minute longer to start being the Church and walking in what it is called to be. The whole Church is called to follow the example of Jesus and to serve one another, to love one another with a sacrificial love. So how can you start living that out now? Where can you serve? What's the job you'd least like to do? Start with that.

The thing about serving is that as much as it outwardly reveals a sense of love and sacrifice, it also does something internally, in our hearts. The act of serving reforms our hearts to be more in line with the heart of God.

In Matthew 20.26–28, Jesus is talking to those in his group who want glory and honour and a place of privilege where they would be revered and served by others and he says:

> **'Instead, whoever wants to become great among you must be your servant, and whoever wants to be first must**

be your slave – just as the Son of Man did not come to be served, but to serve, and to give his life as a ransom for many.'

Jesus came not to be served, but to serve. If you want to grow in your relationship with him and to become more like him, then serving others is a core part of that. In our humanness we sometimes won't want to and our hearts won't be in it like they should be. It's in these moments that our will must call our body to lead our hearts into the service of others. I've often been in the place where I just don't feel like serving, but I've gotten up out of bed and gone anyway, because I don't have to live according to my feelings. I want to live according to the way of Jesus, not the way of Bob Wallington.

#13

USE A GIFT GOD HAS GIVEN YOU

Have you ever done one of those Secret Santa things? You know – the one where a group of you draw each other's names from a hat and buy Christmas gifts for each other? Sometimes I've been part of Secret Santas where part of the 'experience' is that you have to try to guess which of your friends was your Secret Santa after you've opened your present. There's often that weird moment, especially if the gift isn't that great, where you're looking at this thing you've unwrapped, thinking:

1. 'Make it look as if you like the present.'
2. 'Why, in the name of all things holy, has someone given me a milk jug with Donald Trump's face on it as a Christmas present?!'
3. 'Who, out of all these people here, is ridiculous enough to have bought me this?'

Then there can be the awkward, very vulnerable moment when you verbalize who you think bought your present for you. Thinking about it now, it's a situation that is absolutely riddled with potential disaster. With one move I could offend one friend by suggesting she bought my new Donald Trump milk jug and offend another friend for not recognizing his genius comedy and playfulness in the gift before me. Who even thought this thing up?!

In the times when I haven't offended friends and colleagues during the annual Secret Santa gift swap, I have come to notice something interesting. As people unwrap the gift in their hands, they often see something in the gift of the person who bought it for them and sometimes they find out new things about that person too.

As you unwrap the gift, you discover more about the gift giver.

The Bible talks about a whole variety of 'spiritual gifts' that enable us to serve the Church and the world. Most of them can be found in Romans 12, 1 Corinthians 12 and Ephesians 4. They range from gifts of leadership and prophecy to gifts of tongues, wisdom, teaching and evangelism.

1 Corinthians 12.7–11 tells us:

> Now to each one the manifestation of the Spirit is given for the common good. To one there is given through the Spirit a message of wisdom, to another a message of knowledge by means of the same Spirit, to another faith by the same Spirit, to another gifts of healing by that one Spirit, to another miraculous powers, to another prophecy, to another distinguishing between spirits, to another speaking in different kinds of tongues, and to still another the interpretation of tongues. All these are

> **the work of one and the same Spirit, and he distributes them to each one, just as he determines.**

Paul (who is writing this as part of a letter to the church in Corinth) is explaining that each of us is given, through the Holy Spirit, a spiritual gift (or gifts). He doesn't say that some of us have them and others of us need to be a bit more holy before we can have one. We have all been given a spiritual gift and Paul even encourages us to ask God to give us others too.

We can sometimes convince ourselves that we don't have a spiritual gift, but often we just aren't aware yet of what gift God has given us or how to find out which gift we have. This is where I want to encourage you to do two things:

1. pray that God would show you which spiritual gift he has given you;
2. ask people around you – people who know Jesus – what spiritual gift they think God has given you.

In my experience, going on the journey of discovering what gifts God has given you is really exciting! It's like opening a Secret Santa present (which isn't weird!) and working out how to use and operate something brand new that maybe you've never seen before. The best bit is, as you start to discover your gifting and begin the adventure of using it, it draws you closer to the one who gave it to you, it builds your trust in his character, it reveals more of his amazing heart.

The other thing that happens is, as we use, explore and grow in the gifts that God has given us, we not only see and experience more of him but we also become more fully who we were always meant to be. Isn't that amazing?! That God designed and purposed you right from the beginning to be someone who would carry the particular gift he's given you. The gifts aren't just randomly handed out or assigned, but given specifically and intentionally to you.

Paul writes later:

> **Follow the way of love and eagerly desire gifts of the Spirit, especially prophecy . . . the one who prophesies speaks to people for their strengthening, encouraging and comfort . . . I would like every one of you to speak in tongues, but even more to prophesy. (1 Corinthians 14.1, 3, 5)**

What we can take from these verses is that Paul wants us all to ***eagerly*** desire the gifts of the Spirit. They must be an important aspect of living out the Christian faith if Paul is putting such emphasis on them and on us desiring them. He also highlights how important the gift of prophecy is and that it's possible for us all to desire it, receive it and use it.

I grew up in a church where sometimes we would leave space in the service for people to speak out prophetic words that they felt God had spoken to them. They were often linked to prayer, encouraging specific people that God knew them, knew what was going on in their lives and wanted to meet with them by his Spirit as people prayed for them. I remember being totally captivated by this part of the service. I would think, 'WOW! All these people are hearing from God and sometimes it's so specific!'

I remember asking God to speak to me like that. I wanted to hear his voice and his heart and pass it on to people around me. Gradually, each time we made space in the service for prophetic words, I began to feel more confident in what I thought God was saying to me – as if my hearing was getting better. Eventually I started to join in, not every week, but fairly frequently. If I felt God was saying something to me, I would share it out loud and the thing that amazed me most was, sometimes, what I said seemed to connect with people and encourage them to go forwards for prayer.

Each time I saw people respond when I had mustered up the courage to speak out a prophetic word, I felt like my trust in God and connection to him increased a hundred times! It was hard to understand what was going on when no one responded to a prophetic word I had given, but from somewhere God seemed to give me the courage to have another go next time.

As I've got older, I've tried to practise this more and more, not just in church but outside church too. I still feel nervous when I think God is speaking to me or prompting me to do something or to go and speak to someone, but the more I step out and have a go (even though I often don't get it right), the more I see of God's goodness.

A few months ago, our church leaders, Andy and Mike, wrote a fantastic book about some of this stuff. It's called *Everyday Supernatural*.[3] We read it together as a staff team, going through a chapter each week and trying together to step out more when we felt God was speaking, and then to bring back stories each week to encourage one another. I remember after a few weeks thinking that I had listened to quite a few stories that were encouraging, but had not contributed any for myself. So I asked God to give me some opportunities to hear from him and to encourage someone or the church.

It didn't take long. It happened as I was walking out of the main entrance of my local supermarket with some flowers for Tabi. As I was walking into the car park, I noticed an elderly

---

3 Mike Pilavachi and Andy Croft, *Everyday Supernatural* (Eastbourne: David C. Cook, 2016).

lady sitting on a bench to my left. Just like that, a thought popped into my head: 'Give her the flowers.'

'Wow. No,' was my immediate reaction. I walked to my car and put the flowers on the back seat, shut the door and then paused. 'What's the worst that could happen?' I thought. Scenes of her attacking me with her walking stick or handbag raced across my mind, but I thought that maybe I really was meant to give her the flowers.

I walked over to her, holding the flowers and asking God to tell me what to say to her. All I seemed to be able to come up with was the idea that she was not forgotten and God wanted to tell her that he remembered her.

So I sat down next to her (by this time she was looking rather puzzled) and I said something like, 'Excuse me, my name is Bob, I am a Christian and I really think that God wanted me to give these flowers to you and tell you that he hasn't forgotten you.'

She looked utterly stunned, said thank you and told me her name was Margaret. Then she started to cry a little. She explained that she had been in hospital for the past two weeks and had come straight from the hospital to the supermarket in a taxi, because there was no food in her house and she lived alone. Then she said that she had just been sitting there thinking how sad it was that, during the whole two weeks, no one had been able to visit her in hospital and no one had brought her flowers.

My jaw practically hit the floor. I got back in the car rejoicing and thanking God and asking him to use me a million times more like that! (In case you're worried, I went and got Tabi some more flowers.)

So, if you're thinking about exploring this more, here are a couple of suggestions.

3. Ask people whom you trust in your church to pray for you, that you will be filled with the Spirit and that God would show you what gift he has given you or that you would receive a specific gift that God has put on your heart.
3. Keep praying that God would help you grow and develop in that gifting.
4. Try to find opportunities to use that gift. It might be in small amounts at first, but have a go!
5. Find someone in your church who also has that gift and ask them to help you learn how to use and grow in your gift.

Paul reminds us in 1 Corinthians 12, after talking about all kinds of spiritual gifts, that the most excellent of them all is love. These spiritual gifts are most beautifully expressed when they are fuelled by a love for God and a love for people. We won't go far wrong if love is our aim!

#14

FIND 15 MINUTES TO STOP AND PRAY EACH WEEK

I once heard the story of a guy whose dad used to wake him up almost every day in the same way: he would come into his room, pull back the curtains, turn to his son and say, 'Morning, son! God is still on the throne and prayer changes things.' Then he would disappear and let his son wake up and start the day with those words ringing in his ears.

That definitely beats the old wooden spoon and saucepan clapping that I sometimes experienced to chase me into my school uniform and out the door!

But imagine that for a moment (aside from the fact that you're being woken up): imagine starting each day being reminded that the God you love and worship and follow is in the most significant place of power that exists in every world, universe, realm and dimension. Your God, your Father, is reigning in power AND, when you speak to him, stuff happens.

For some reason, those are not always my first thoughts when I think about prayer. I come at prayer from the angle that says, 'Errr . . . please, Father, if you wouldn't mind, I could do with . . . err . . . some of your power . . . no . . . just a bit, if you could spare it . . . because there's this thing and it's quite important . . . Well, I'm not sure if it's important to you, but it's important to me . . . Wait . . . are you there? Are you listening? Well, if you are, could you help me in my maths exam today . . . Thanks.'

Sometimes I pray, but I forget who I'm praying to. I mean, I know it's God, but I just forget what he's like and who he is and where he is and the infinite power that is his and is available at my request. I sometimes subconsciously doubt that he will answer my prayers or those of others because it appears that, on various occasions, he may not have in the past.

I also forget that Jesus, in communicating God's heart, told his disciples to ask God (in prayer) for everything they needed and God would respond as a good father would.

> 'Ask and it will be given to you; seek and you will find; knock and the door will be opened to you. For everyone who asks receives; the one who seeks finds; and to the one who knocks, the door will be opened.
>
> 'Which of you, if your son asks for bread, will give him a stone? Or if he asks for a fish, will give him a snake? If you, then, though you are evil, know how to give good gifts to your children, how much more will your Father in heaven give good gifts to those who ask him!' (Matthew 7.7–11)

The other thing I forget is we live in a world that is at war spiritually. We go about our everyday lives, at school, college or work, and forget so often that we are spiritual beings and all around us, but beyond what we can see, there is a war being waged and we are right in the middle of it.

Paul wrote to the Ephesians (chapter 6) and said to them that there was a war on and it wasn't a battle against flesh and blood, but against the spiritual powers of this world (the devil and his pals). One of the key tactics that the devil and his pals have used against us is to convince us there is no war and he and his minions don't actually exist. The enemy uses many ways to do this and one of the most effective is to make us comfortable and make us busy. The comfort we think we enjoy is a veil covering the reality that we are at war, but the comfort feels . . . well, comfortable and nice and, when we feel comfortable and at peace, we pray less. The busyness that so many of us experience is a way of distracting us from the main thing. When our consciousness is constantly bombarded with other things that are 'more important', suddenly we don't have time to pray, even if we wanted to. We're too busy to pray. Eugene Peterson once said, 'Busyness is the enemy of spirituality.'[4]

Have you ever trodden on a nail? I have. I was playing in a friend's garden when I was about eight or nine years old and we were jumping all over a wood pile at the bottom of his

4 Eugene H. Peterson, *Subversive Spirituality* (Grand Rapids, MI: Eerdmans Publishing, 1997).

garden, making forts and pretending to be soldiers. After a whole afternoon playing outside, we came in to my friend's house and took our shoes off (we had been incredibly well trained). I looked at what should have been a white sock on my foot and it was soaked in blood. I freaked out! What had happened?!

At some stage in the afternoon I had trodden on a nail. It had almost gone right through my foot, but I hadn't felt it because it had been in the middle of the game, while we were running about, and my whole focus had been on something else.

Sometimes, when it comes to the spiritual war that we each find ourselves in, the busyness of life can distract us from the reality that we're under attack, to the extent that we don't even think we are. Then comes a moment when something happens: we take off a shoe and find a blood-soaked sock and realize that things are not as we thought they were.

So, to recap, the main reasons I don't pray are:

- I lose sight of who I am praying to and his invitation to ask;
- I forget that I am in the middle of a spiritual battle;
- life is just very, very busy.

You might have reasons similar to mine that get in the way of you praying or you might have different ones. Some of my friends struggle with prayer because they sometimes doubt that it makes any difference at all or they've really prayed about certain situations in the past and it doesn't seem like anything has changed (more about this in the next chapter).

What can we do, then? Well, I want to suggest one very small, but very difficult, practice that you can build into your life to help you begin the journey and draw you deeper into relationship with Jesus . . .

Stop. For 15 minutes. Once a week. And pray.

When I say that, it sounds like such a small amount of time. Fifteen measly minutes out of my whole week to stop and pray?! That's it?

Yes!

Well, it's the beginning. It's the beginning of fighting back and taking back what's been stolen and getting your head back in the game. It's going to be the moment when you remind yourself what's really going on in the world around you and that you can do something to bring light into a world which sometimes feels very dark.

The thing is, as we spend time praying, we get more passionate about praying and we see the power in our prayers. Spending time in the presence of God, speaking to him and also listening to him, naturally draws us closer to him and deepens our relationship with him.

So . . . where are those 15 minutes in your life? Have a look at your weekly schedule and try to find a slot where you can give 15 minutes to remind yourself of the invitation that has been extended to you to ask, seek and knock, to remind yourself of who it is that you are praying to and that there is nothing impossible for him. When will you find that moment to remind yourself you are in a battle and the enemy is continually trying to keep you so busy you can't get in the battle?

It's time to get in the fight.

#15

ASK THREE PEOPLE TO PRAY FOR YOU EVERY DAY

When I was growing up, there was an older couple who lived at the top of our street. They were called Arthur and Shirley and they were amazing. Arthur was bald and, for as long as I can remember, suffered from Parkinson's disease. He also had the best sense of humour of anyone I knew (he once let us cover his head in squirty cream while we were all eating dessert at Youth Alpha!) Shirley was a well of encouragement, positivity and support, and she had the biggest smile around.

These two prayed for me a lot. I knew they did and it made a massive difference in my life to know that there were people (aside from family members) who were praying for me pretty much every day. I felt more secure, more free to be me, more expectant for God to move in my life.

A few years ago, when I was working with the amazing team at Onelife (who work to raise up, encourage and inspire young leaders), we were hosting a conference for young leaders. One of the older ladies in the congregation of the host church asked to have a list of the names of all the delegates who were coming, so that she could pray for each of them as they attended the conference. We found out that she was still praying every day for each person on the list a year later.

The Power of Prayer

I wonder sometimes if we underestimate the power of prayer. Watchman Nee, a twentieth-century Chinese church leader and teacher, wrote:

Our prayers lay the track down which God's power can come. Like a mighty locomotive, his power is irresistible, but it cannot reach us without rails.[5]

If we understood more about how powerful prayer is, we would all pray more. I have no doubt that one of Satan's key strategies is to convince us our prayers (and prayer in general) are ineffective, that when you and I ask, seek and knock, for some reason our petitions are either not heard or not responded to. The truth is that God (despite the outcome of our prayers) hears our cries to him and he is sovereign over everything, with power greater than we could ever grasp or imagine. We don't always understand his ways or why some things happen and other things don't happen, but the Bible calls us to lift our eyes above what we can see and understand, to fix them on who God is.

I'm not saying that's easy. I have found myself, at many points in my life, wondering if God can hear me or if he somehow

5 Watchman Nee, *The Collected Works of Watchman* Nee (Anaheim, CA: Living Stream Ministry, 1992–1994).

doesn't care about the people I love or the things they are going through. As I look back on those moments of utter loss and despair, I choose to believe that God is my Father and he is the truest form of goodness, that his love for me and for every person I have ever met is so great, he would sacrifice his only Son to the most brutal of deaths in order to reach out his hand to us and draw us into an everlasting embrace of love.

I don't understand God. But when the chips are down, I trust in his love.

If you're wondering whether or not God is listening to your prayers, you're in good company! King David felt like this too sometimes. Psalm 13 shows us his approach to unanswered prayer and suffering:

> How long, LORD? Will you forget me for ever?
> How long will you hide your face from me?
> How long must I wrestle with my thoughts
> and day after day have sorrow in my heart?
> How long will my enemy triumph over me?
> Look on me and answer, LORD my God.
> Give light to my eyes, or I will sleep in death,
> and my enemy will say, 'I have overcome him,'
> and my foes will rejoice when I fall.
> But I trust in your unfailing love;
> my heart rejoices in your salvation.

I will sing the LORD's praise,
for he has been good to me.

I think we sometimes forget very quickly about the prayers that do get answered. I mean, I'm sure we often remember the big ones, but the small prayers we may send up during the day that get answered, I think we are quick to forget (that's why #5, 'Record the Story', is important!) If I think about it, I think I have experienced God answering my prayers a lot more than not answering them.

As I mentioned earlier, a few years ago I took a team of 16 young people to Uganda in Africa to run conferences for young Ugandan leaders. I was nervous before we left for Uganda, as I was responsible for everyone. If anything were to go wrong, it would ultimately be up to me to sort it – and sorting things in a country you don't know very well (especially if it's a medical problem or some other kind of emergency) can be quite difficult!

I prayed a lot before the trip. I prayed for safety, for our health, for the conferences, for the young people attending, for the flights, the connections, the finances, the accommodation. I prayed for lots of different aspects of the trip and God answered SO MANY of my prayers!! I mentioned in a previous chapter the lady who was deaf in one ear and, when my friend Zoe and I prayed for her, it was completely healed. On that same day, a heavily pregnant lady came to us on the same street and asked us to pray that she would go into labour very soon. Her baby was well overdue and she was worried that the size of the baby could lead to serious complications. Some of our team prayed for her and we found out the next day that she basically walked back to her house, went into labour and had the baby that evening.

Of course, I remember the miracles like that. The signs and wonders that display the goodness, power and love of God are hard to forget, but the hundreds of other answered prayers I experienced before and during that trip somehow seem to float out of my conscious memory.

What I'm trying to illustrate here is that I believe God answers far more prayers than we give him credit for or remember. Sometimes the painful, seemingly unanswered, prayers sit so heavily in our consciousness that the enemy uses them to write a script in our minds that repeats over and over, which says, 'God doesn't answer your prayers.'

But the truth that we need to remember is he does.

The Bible backs this up in many places, but one of my favourite verses about prayer is James 5.16, which says, 'The prayer of a righteous person is powerful and effective.'

Being Surrounded by Prayer . . . Every Day!

Now let's take this understanding of prayer and apply it to what this chapter is really all about. Wouldn't it be amazing to have people in your life who you knew were praying powerful and effective prayers for you and on your behalf every single day? So instead of thinking, 'It's just me praying,' you can walk into each day knowing that several other people are praying for you too, and that their prayers are powerful!

For me, growing up knowing that my friends Arthur and Shirley were praying for me every day gave me a sense of belief that I was being strengthened and supported in a way that other people (who didn't have a relationship with Jesus) were not. I felt like I was a foot taller. There was a God-given confidence in me because Arthur and Shirley were praying for me.

I wonder if your church has quite a few older people in it? Maybe it's a church of much younger people. On the whole, most churches I go into these days have a healthy number of older people. While every now and again older people and younger people can rub each other up the wrong way, in my experience older people will usually jump at the chance to be someone in your life who prays for you every day. A lot of the time, older people have much to teach us about prayer.

But it doesn't have to be someone who's older than you who you ask to pray for you every day. It could be a friend in the youth group or maybe even someone who's a lot younger than you. It could be a youth leader or a godparent or – heaven forbid – your own parents or carers!

So here's the challenge: find three people and ask them if they would be willing to pray for you every day. Maybe ask them if there's anything that would be helpful to them as they pray. Some might like to know if there's anything specific they can pray for. Others might just like to know a bit more information about you to help them pray (such as if you are enjoying school or what you're hoping to do in the future).

Find those three people. Ask them to pray for you every day and see what a difference it makes in your life and in your relationship with Jesus.

God is on the throne and prayer changes things.

#16

PRAY FOR TEN FRIENDS/ FAMILY EVERY DAY

I don't know if you've ever heard of a man called Dwight Lyman Moody? Some may have heard of him as D. L. Moody. He was born in 1837 in Massachusetts in the USA. His dad was a farmer and his mum raised Dwight and his eight brothers and sisters. He attended church during his childhood, but at the age of 17, he heard for the first time about the love that God had for him and he gave his life to Jesus.

D. L. Moody became one of the most famous evangelists of his time and led many people to Jesus. One of the stories I love most about him is that at some stage in his life he made a list of a hundred people he knew who didn't know Jesus. He resolved to pray for them every day. By the time D. L. Moody died in 1899, 96 people on his list had given their lives to Jesus. Not bad going! But the even more amazing thing is that the other four people on his list became Christians at his funeral!

When I hear stories like that, I feel encouraged to embark on the adventure of asking, seeking and knocking on the door of heaven for God to soften the hearts of people in my life who don't yet know him.

The truth is that God is the only one who can do this. But there is a part for us to play too! We are invited into this adventure primarily through prayer.

I often wish I was better at arguing a case for the gospel, at explaining why I believe it to be true to those who state it can't be. I wish I was able to perform great signs and wonders so that people would have no choice but to fall to their knees and acknowledge Jesus Christ as Lord. I wish I could preach so eloquently that hearts and minds would bow effortlessly before the King of Kings. Although I might wish for all these things, what I can do in the here and now is to pray.

I can pray like a dripping tap. Over and over and over again. I can pray with heart, because I love and care for the people I am praying for and I desperately want them to know the love of God. I can pray with passion and vision to see the lives of those people to be transformed by coming into relationship with Jesus. I can pray even when I feel like nothing is happening, because I choose to see, in faith, a different reality from the one my eyes receive.

What if you and I were to write our own lists, like D. L. Moody did?

A hundred seems like a mighty big number, so what if, instead, we were to write a list of ten? Ten people who are in our lives who don't know Jesus yet. Some of them might be family members, friends or people we work with; they could be people we see every day or people we see once a year;

people we know really well or people that we only know a little. Why don't you write a list?

Now you might be reading this and thinking, 'Yes, lovely idea, but what does that have to do with me deepening my relationship with God? That's all about other people, right?' You would have a valid point. On the surface, praying for our friends and family to know the love of God doesn't seem like it would have much of an immediate effect on us.

But it does. Here's why.

When you pray through your list every day, you'll get a bit bored of praying, 'I pray that Daniel comes to faith, I pray that Gemma comes to faith, I pray that Asher comes to faith' and so on. What will probably happen after a while is that you will want to change it up a bit or look for other ways to pray for the people on your list to come to know Jesus, and that's where it becomes really powerful for us as we pray. Because that will make us think about the relationship we have with Jesus and what being a Christian means to us on the inside. We'll start to pray a bit more like this: 'Dear Father, I know Daniel needs you right now. He's going through such a tough time at home with his dad walking out on the family. He needs a father. He needs to know you as his heavenly Father. Please show yourself to Daniel, Lord.'

As we pray for our friends and family to come into relationship with God, we remind ourselves of what being in relationship with God has given us.

Another way it will grow you in your relationship with God is that, when the people on your list start becoming Christians, you will go bananas! By that I mean you will love it and it will be incredibly encouraging! Imagine D. L. Moody by the time 96 of his list had become Christians! He must have been absolutely overjoyed and more aware of the power of his prayers than ever.

Seeing the people we love and have been praying for come into relationship with God is just the best. It fills us with a greater sense of joy and faith for even more.

For many years now, I've taken groups of young people to the Soul Survivor festivals during the summer in the UK. One of the things I've loved most is that there are always several opportunities given for the young people to make a decision to come into relationship with God for the first time. Over the years, young people have often brought friends along who aren't Christians, praying that they would at some stage hear the good news about Jesus, believe it and give their lives to him, and the amazing thing is that it happens again and again and again, every year.

At the festivals, the young people who want to give their lives to Jesus are usually invited to stand up (in front of eight or nine thousand other young people) and asked to make their way to the front of the giant tent or arena, where they gather in front of the stage. Obviously, this can be rather intimidating, so they often bring a friend with them to lessen that feeling! I can usually tell which one the friend is, because he or she is often the one beaming from ear to ear, practically skipping along. On more than one occasion I've seen a whole youth group get up and go forwards with one of their number who is giving their life to Jesus! We get excited when our prayers are answered. We celebrate when those for whom we have been praying to receive the love of God receive it. The Bible tells us that there is rejoicing in heaven, even when one person repents and comes into relationship with Jesus.

I long for those people on my list to know and experience the love of God, to know the 'amazing grace' that we sing about, to be in relationship with the one who breathed them into being and on whose hands their name is written. I may or may not have opportunities to speak to them about Jesus or chances here and there to show them the love of God through my actions, but I will always be able to pray for them.

Make your list, and pray, pray, pray!

#16½

SET YOUR YOUTH GROUP ON FIRE

I wonder if you've ever believed that you could make a difference to your youth group. Is it possible that you could make an impact, that something you do could change what your youth group is like? The truth is that you can, even if you're the only person in it at the moment!

Not many young people have approached me in my 16 years of working in youth ministry to ask what they could do to take the youth group to the next level. I wonder if that's because many young people don't realize the potential they have to make a difference. I've had quite a few young people (and their parents) share with me their ideas about what *I* could do to make a positive impact on the youth group and take it to the next level, but not very many young people ask me what *they* could do.

When I read the book of Acts (especially the first few chapters), my heart is filled with excitement at what happened when God took an ordinary bunch of young people (it's thought the disciples were teenagers when Jesus first called them), gave them a mission and then filled them with the Holy Spirit. I often dream of what it would be like to see the young people of my church set on fire in the same way. What would we see happening in our community, our schools, our church?

What do you think that would be like in your church, school, college, community, university or city?

From what I know of God and what I've seen in his word, I don't think that my youth group has explored all there is to explore of God, nor taken hold of everything that we have been given in order that we might see the kingdom of heaven touching earth. (I include myself in that.) There is so much more of God than we have currently discovered, and so much more for us to understand and enter into in order to see his kingdom come in greater power.

I'm not sure that we have even begun to scratch the surface of what is possible. I read the words of Jesus that we would do even greater things than he did (John 14.12) and I feel dissatisfied that we're not there yet, but buoyed with hope that there is SO MUCH MORE for us, his children, to take hold of and claim in his name. My deepest longing is to see his kingdom on earth as it is in heaven; to see with my own eyes heaven touching earth; to behold the beautiful, all-loving power of God and his salvation come like a flood into the lives of everyone I know.

So what can you do? How can you make a difference?

I think it starts with the desire to see more of God's presence at work in your life and in the lives of your friends in your youth group. That passion can fuel and propel you into action and help you persevere when you don't think anything is changing.

But the fundamental truth that you need to hold on to here is: you can make a difference.

I love reading accounts of revivals (times when God's Spirit has moved in places with incredible power) that have happened in the past and trying to imagine what they were like. When God has moved like this in the past, what has usually been seen is loads of people coming to know Jesus for the first time. In some cases, people have been saved in their hundreds and thousands. Some stories of revivals in Scotland and Wales tell of people falling to their knees in the streets and in the fields to repent of their sins (without anyone preaching a word to them) and asking Jesus to come into their lives as Lord.

One of my favourite stories is of the revival on the Isle of Lewes, just off the coast of Scotland, in 1949. A man named Duncan Campbell was invited to the island to preach in the church because some of the congregation felt that God was about to do something powerful. When the first evening meeting ended, where about 300 people were in attendance, it didn't seem like anything particularly different had happened. Then a man from the congregation, desperate for God to work, cried out to God aloud and begged for the Holy Spirit to move. Duncan Campbell wrote of what happened next:

> Soon he is on his knees in the aisle and he is still praying and then he falls into a trance again. Just then the door opened – it is now eleven o'clock. The door of the church opens and the local blacksmith comes back into the church and says, 'Mr. Campbell, something wonderful has happened. Oh, we were praying that God would pour water on the thirsty and floods upon the dry ground and listen, He's done it! He's done it!'
>
> When I went to the door of the church I saw a congregation of approximately 600 people. Six hundred people – where had they come from? What had happened? I believe that that very night God swept in in Pentecostal power – the power of the Holy Ghost. And what happened in the early days of the apostles was happening now in the parish of Barvas.
>
> Over 100 young people were at the dance in the parish hall and they weren't thinking of God or eternity. God was not in all of their thoughts. They were there to have a good night when suddenly the power of God fell upon the dance. The music ceased and in a matter of minutes, the hall was empty. They fled from the hall as a man fleeing from a plague. And they made for the church. They are now

standing outside. Oh, yes – they saw lights in the church. That was a house of God and they were going to it and they went. Men and women who had gone to bed rose, dressed, and made for the church. Nothing in the way of publicity . . . But God took the situation in hand – oh, He became His own publicity agent. A hunger and a thirst gripped the people. 600 of them now are at the church standing outside . . . And then the doors were opened and the congregation flocked back into the church.

Now the church is crowded – a church to seat over 800 is now packed to capacity. It is now going on towards midnight. I managed to make my way through the crowd along the aisle toward the pulpit. I found a young woman, a teacher in the grammar school, lying prostrate on the floor of the pulpit praying, 'Oh, God, is there mercy for me? Oh, God, is there mercy for me?' She was one of those at the dance. But she is now lying on the floor of the pulpit crying to God for mercy.

That meeting continued until 4 o'clock in the morning. So we left them there, and just as I was leaving the church, a young man came to me and said, 'Mr. Campbell, I would like you to go to the police station.' I said, 'The police station? What's wrong?' 'Oh,' he said, 'There's nothing wrong but there must be at least 400 people gathered around the police station just now.'

Now the sergeant there was a God-fearing man. He was in the meeting. But people knew that this was a house that feared God. And next to the police station was the cottage in which the two old women lived. I believe that that had something to do with the magnet, the power that drew men. There was a coach load at that meeting. A coach load had come over 12 miles to be there. Now if anyone would ask them today, why? How did it happen? Who arranged it? They couldn't tell you. But they found themselves grouping together and someone saying, 'What about going to Barvas? I don't know, but I have a hunger in my heart to go there.' I can't explain it; they couldn't explain it, but God had the situation in hand.

This is revival dear people! This is a sovereign act of God! This is the moving of God's Spirit, I believe in answer to the prevailing prayer of men and women who believed that God was a covenant-keeping God but must be true to His covenant engagement . . .

That continued for almost 3 years. Until the whole of the island was swept by the mighty power of God.[6]

---

6 Duncan Campbell, 'Revival in the Hebrides (1949)', *Christians Together In the Highlands and Islands* (available online at: <www.christianstogether.net/Articles/94936/Christians_Together_in/Christian_Life/Revival_in_the.aspx> (accessed 20 February 2019).

Accounts of revivals like this fill me with a deep longing that God would move again in power in my lifetime! But the thing I love most about this particular revival is that, long before it happened, there were two elderly ladies who lived on the island of Lewes who were saddened by the state of people's hearts on their island and how far away from the love of God they seemed. The two ladies, one of them 82 and the other 84 years old and blind, decided that they would pray every Tuesday night in their tiny little cottage for God to do something that they could not. They prayed from 10.00 o'clock in the evening until 3.00 or 4.00 a.m. in the morning, sometimes twice a week.

I'm challenged when I read about those two elderly ladies. I'm challenged by their desperation to see things change and for heaven to touch earth. I'm challenged because they didn't just assume things had to be the way they were. I'm challenged that they were willing to give up sleep (and elderly people need their sleep!) to bang on the doors of heaven for God to move.

We need God in our day, just as desperately as those two elderly ladies knew they needed God in theirs. I wonder if we're desperate enough that we might get on our knees and pray to ask God to send his Spirit in power on our youth groups.

> **The greatest need of the church, and the thing which, above all others, believers ought to seek for with one**

> **mind and with their whole heart, is to be filled with the Spirit of God.**[7]

Why Is this Half a Chapter?

I numbered this chapter 16½ as a reminder that you and I don't have half of what is necessary to set a youth group on fire. No matter how hard we try, work and graft, we still won't be able to do it on our own. All we can do is offer the little that we do have and the little we can do and trust everything else to God. God is, and has, the power and the truth is that, without him, we have nothing. Jesus said to his disciples:

> **'I am the vine; you are the branches. If you remain in me and I in you, you will bear much fruit; apart from me you can do nothing.' (John 15.5)**

This has been the end goal of every chapter in this book. Each practical act that we can engage in to 'upgrade' our faith is actually all about drawing us closer to and rooting us deeper in the vine. It is God himself who is going to grow us, to change us more into his likeness, and each of these

---

[7] Andrew Murray, *The Believer's Full Blessing of Pentecost* (Bloomington, MN: Bethany House Publishers, 1984).

practical tips aims to set us at his feet, with our hearts open and surrendered to him.

The more we draw closer to God, the more we see and experience his great love for us, the more we, in turn, love him. It's love that changes us.

> **See what great love the Father has lavished on us, that we should be called children of God! And that is what we are! (1 John 3.1)**

Here are a few things you could do to help set your youth group on fire.

1. Set aside some time regularly to pray that God would move in power in your youth group. You could even do this with a friend or a group of friends.
2. Turn up consistently to your youth group and come with an attitude to invest, not purely receive.
3. If there are times of worship (sung worship or other kinds), model what it looks like to throw your whole self into it.
4. Pray for your leaders.

RESOURCES

Here are some resources that had a massive impact on me growing up or I have gained from reading since and I commend them to you.

Books

Easy, captivating reads:

- Brother Andrew, *God's Smuggler* (Hodder & Stoughton, 2008)
- Nicky Cruz, *The Cross and the Switchblade* (Zondervan, 2002)
- Mike Pilavachi and Andy Croft, *Storylines* (Kingsway, 2010)
- Mike Pilavachi and Andy Croft, *Lifelines* (David C. Cook, 2018)
- Jackie Pullinger, *Chasing the Dragon* (Hodder & Stoughton, 2006)
- dc Talk, *Jesus Freaks* (Honor Books, 1995)

Inspiration for going deeper with God:

- Shane Claibourne, *The Irresistible Revolution* (Zondervan, 2006)
- Mike Foster, *Freeway: A not-so-perfect guide to freedom* (SecondChance.org, 2013)

- Mike Foster, *Wonderlife: A not-so-perfect guide to who you are and why you're here* (SecondChance.org, 2016)
- Timothy Keller, *Encounters with Jesus* (Hodder & Stoughton, 2014)
- Mike Pilavachi, *Wasteland?* (Kingsway, 2003)
- Mike Pilavachi with Liza Hoeksma, *Worship, Evangelism, Justice* (Kingsway, 2006)
- Matt Redman, *Facedown* (Kingsway, 2004)
- Vaughan Roberts, *God's Big Picture* (IVP, 2017)

Books to help you explore your relationship with the Holy Spirit:

- Chris Lane, *Ordinary Miracles* (Instant Apostle, 2017)
- Jeannie Morgan, *Encounter the Holy Spirit* (Monarch, 2011)
- Jeannie Morgan, *Our Hands, His Healing* (Monarch, 2014)
- Mike Pilavachi and Andy Croft, *Everyday Supernatural* (David C. Cook, 2016)
- John Wimber with Kevin Springer, *Power Evangelism* (Hodder & Stoughton, 2013)

Harder to read, but SO GOOD:

- Richard Foster, *Celebration of Discipline* (Hodder & Stoughton, 2008)
- Watchman Nee, *The Normal Christian Life* (Clc Publications, 2009)
- J. I. Packer, *Knowing God* (Hodder & Stoughton, 2005)
- Dallas Willard, *The Divine Conspiracy* (William Collins, 2014)

Help with Chapter 6, Clear the Road Block:

- Rachel Gardner, *The Girl De-Construction Project* (Hodder & Stoughton, 2018)
- Catherine Price, *How to Break up with Your Phone* (Trapeze, 2019)
- Jack Skett, *A Better Kind of Intimacy* (Instant Apostle, 2018)

Websites and Blogs

Alpha Youth Series Asking questions about faith: <https://alpha.org/alpha-youth-series>

Crowned UK Inspiring girls in faith, life and identity: <https://crowneduk.co.uk>

Mind The mental health charity: <www.mind.org.uk>

More Precious Equipping girls' relationship with God: <www.moreprecious.co.uk>

Reboot Asking big questions about faith: <www.rebootglobal.org>

Romance Academy <www.romanceacademy.org>

Selfharm UK <www.selfharm.co.uk>

Think Twice Aims to assist those struggling with mental illness and those who stand beside them: <www.thinktwiceinfo.org>

Music

Bethel Music, *Victory* (Bethel Music, 2019)

Joe Bright, *Rhythms and Sweet Symphony* (Joe Bright, 2016 and 2018)

Beth Croft, *Rule in My Heart* (Integrity Music, 2014)
Guvna B, *Hands Are Made for Working* (Allo Mate Records, 2018)
Hillsong UNITED, *Of Dirt and Grace and Wonder* (Hillsong Music, 2016 and 2017)
Hillsong Young and Free, *III*, Live at Hillsong Conference (Absolute, 2018)
Jeremy Riddle, *More* (Bethel Music, 2017)
Tom Smith, *Everyday* (Integrity Music, 2018)
Soul Survivor *Standing on the Edge* (Integrity Music, 2018)
Phil Wickham, *Living Hope* (Fair Trade Services, 2018)
Worship Central, *Stir a Passion* (Integrity Music, 2018)

YouTube

Soul Survivor Great interviews, talks and more about how to live for Jesus.
The Bible Project Brilliant content to help you improve your understanding of the Bible.

Journaling

The Soul Survivor Journaling Bible (Hodder & Stoughton, 2019)